DEBT FRE[

MASTERPLAN:

Rapidly Get Out Of Debt, Build Wealth & Master Money Management - Proven Strategies To Save Money, Pay Off Your Credit Card, Beat Bad Credit & Stop Compulsive Spending Addiction

Table of Contents

Introduction

Congratulations on taking the first step towards recovering from the terrible cycle of debt. It takes a lot of strength to decide to make the necessary changes needed to recover from debt and to change your financial habits for the better. You should be proud of yourself for making this choice.

What this introduction will do is serve as a layout for all that you will be discovering as you progress through this book. It will also explain the layout of each chapter. Getting out of debt does not happen overnight but making some changes can happen instantly!

The goal of this book is to offer you a set of tools, tips, and tricks to help you regain control of your finances and get you out of debt. Part of how I will do that is by finishing each chapter with a series of "homework" assignments. The goal of the assignments is to get you actively changing and working on your debt as you move through the book.

The homework is by no means required, but many of the questions or tasks will help you come to terms with your own finances and understand what led you to this state or what mindsets cause you to spend and save the way you do. Some assignments will require writing out answers to questions, but others will ask only that you try new things. The key is to be open to learning more about yourself as you move through this book.

Let's talk about the chapters and their order. To start with, I will be giving you advice on breaking out of debt and saving money. This is the first chapter because it will guide you in immediately jumping out of the cycle of debt. There is no way you can solve your debt problems until you actually stop the habits that keep you in debt. For those who don't fully understand debt, you'll also learn about good versus bad debt and why debt is necessary. We'll end the chapter with advice on starting your own small savings account for emergencies to prevent going into further debt because of unexpected situations.

Once you break out of the debt cycle, you move on to chapter two. Chapter two is all about finding out just how much you know regarding your own finances and debt. This chapter will help you get an idea of what information you need to create a new budget and debt repayment plan. You'll be asked to find out exactly who you owe money to and how much you owe. This is where breaking out of debt gets very real. You will need to acknowledge just how in debt you truly are.

Chapter three is the beginning stage in the process of changing your financial habits for the better. This chapter focuses on presenting a series of "do's" and "don'ts" that relate to your spending, your budgeting, your debt repayment, and how you take on more debt. It is an extensive list, but most are easy to make changes. Once you know them, you can begin changing your habits on a daily basis for the better.

After checking your own habits against the do's and don'ts of chapter three, you will need to move on to the topic of your "mindset". Just like you needed to understand your own debt and financial situation, you also need to take a good hard look at your mindsets regarding money and finances. Chapter four will analyze your views regarding money. If you don't have helpful views around money, you are not going to be able to be successful in repaying your debts and breaking the cycle. We'll give you some easy to follow advice on changing your views regarding money and budgeting.

After you begin working on your mindset and shaping your gratitude practice, you will move into chapter five where you will be given a series of major money mistakes many people have made. This chapter is all about recognizing those mistakes and learning ways to avoid making them. It is essential that you have the tools to succeed, but I cannot give those to you without also warning you about easy to make mistakes when it comes to finances.

Chapter eight is equally as important as the list of don'ts and the list of money mistakes. This chapter is focused entirely on the secrets of the wealthy. People who are wealthy make the right choices to remain healthy and to grow their empire. In chapter eight you'll get a list of tips that the wisest wealthy people follow.

As you move into chapter nine, you will have a full set of tools at your ready. Chapter nine is one of the most important chapters in this book. It is where you will learn all about budgeting. You will be guided in how to make a budget from start to finish, along with being given tips that help you make your budget successful and easy to follow, along with a list of mistakes many people make when they begin budgeting. There will be some resources to help you find the best budgeting process for you.

After reading chapter ten you will have your own budget to work with. But having a budget alone isn't going to lead to success and good habits. Once you have a budget you also need to look at your spending. Chapter eleven is all about mastering your spending. You will be given guidance to help you make the right choices when you spend your money.

Finally, given that getting out of debt is based on making a good income and spending that income wisely, chapter eleven is all about finding extra ways to boost your income. We will give you a lengthy list of potential opportunities for you to make money both online and locally. This will be good for those of you who have only a small amount of money to put towards debt repayment. You could be making $100 to $200 just taking surveys while watching television for example!

At the end of these chapters you will head into the conclusion of the book where we will recap some of the most important points from each chapter. You'll be given a set of homework tasks to walk away with upon completing this book, along with some resources to help you continue building your healthy financial habits.

Now here comes the important part! Your homework:

If you are ready to commit, and you feel like this book will be helpful, it is time to complete your first important task: signing this contract!

I, _____, reader of *The Debt Free Masterplan* commit to taking the necessary steps towards bettering my financial life and getting out of debt. Today, on the _____ day of the month of _____ in the year of _____ I am choosing to begin this journey of breaking out of the debt cycle, changing my financial habits for the better, and beginning the process of repaying my debts. I commit to being open, to being honest, and to trying out the advice recommended to me as best as I can.

_____ will be my accountability partner and will be the person I can check in with to let them know how I am doing in my debt repayment plan. My goal is to be debt free in _____ years and I will do what I can to achieve this goal.

(Insert applause)

If you have signed the contract, then congratulations. You have taken the first step and you are ready to begin your masterplan journey. Let's move on then, shall we?

Breaking the cycle of debt. How can I start saving now?

Here's what you'll learn in this chapter:

1. **What is the difference between good and bad debt?**
2. **What is the debt cycle and how do we break it?**
3. **The importance of an emergency fund.**
4. **Easy ways to start an emergency fund today.**
5. **What changes can I make right now?**

How many of you wake up each morning and the first thing on your mind is what bill is due today? Or maybe you wake up and wonder if you will have enough money to join your coworkers at the bar for a Friday night happy hour? Or maybe it's even simpler, maybe you wake up and check your bank account only to see you only have a few digits of available funds. Debt is vicious. It is a toll that weighs heavily on most people and it can cause a great deal of stress in our daily lives.

Well I'm here to tell you that living in debt doesn't have to be a permanent thing. Debt is a cycle, but that doesn't mean you have to remain stuck in it year after year. The cycle of debt, like all other cycles, can be broken. It can be done using easy to understand tools, easy to follow steps, and by making the right choices in regard to spending and saving. But before we go any further, let's begin by defining some of these concepts.

What is debt? Is all debt bad?

Debt is typically defined as something that is owed or due. While this may sound like a bad thing, it is not always negative to have debt. Debt is part of our everyday lives. Without taking on debt many people would not be able to own homes, attend college, or start businesses. Debt allows us to pursue things we would not be able to if we had to fund them ourselves upfront. In addition, taking on debt in early adulthood is part of how we learn to establish and create good credit so that we can qualify for other things later in life like a home or a car.

While there are many helpful debts, there are a lot more harmful debts. Credit cards can often be more harmful than good. Some companies offer outrageous interest rates to people who are getting a card for the first time. Some cards require you pay back much more over time which makes it difficult to absolutely diminish the debt. Some school loans can be helpful, but others create interest that adds up even while you're in school. These types of debt can make it difficult to ultimately be debt free.

If you've made any of the above choices, do not think you are totally hopeless. This book is here to help you get control of your debt and to learn how to avoid making costly mistakes in the future.

What is a debt cycle?

When we originally take on debt, we do it with the intent of paying it back. Now most debt comes with interest charges which causes us to usually pay back more than what was originally borrowed. A debt cycle occurs when we take on debt we can't repay with an interest rate that is too high to manage. We find ourselves overwhelmed by how much we owe. Many people then turn to more debt to help solve this problem.

Let's say for example, you open a credit card to fund a short-term need, like textbooks for college or to afford a vacation you really want to take. Ideally, we would make payments on this until it is paid back. Sometimes however, people take on more debt than they can manage which means they use the credit card. Then they make the payment, but then they keep using the credit card. This can become even more damaging when people begin resorting to pay day loans or similar high interest quick solutions that cause more harm than good.

Sometimes debt cycles happen beyond our control. Like in the case of people taking out loans to cover medical expenses or unplanned for emergencies. Just because a person is caught in a debt cycle doesn't mean they should feel guilty. It happens to people all around the world every day. But that is why I'm here to help. By following actionable steps, making smart choices, and being honest with yourself, it is entirely possible to break the debt cycle.

Breaking the debt cycle

Like most situations or problems in our life, the first step is to admit that you are trapped in a debt cycle. Only after acknowledging that changes need to happen can you then begin learning and implementing those changes. This is not a time to beat yourself up either, instead accept the reality and focus on the future. Once you've accepted the truth about your situation in regard to your finances, it is time to get a clear understanding of your financial situation by making sure you know each of the following:

1. What is your income like? Do you have a set income that you bring home each week, each month, twice a month? Do you have an income that changes based on hours worked, or based on the season? People who work seasonal jobs such as teachers, or those who earn income in blocks like college students, need to have a different spending and savings plan than those who don't.

2. What are your absolutely necessary expenses each month? Once you have a clear idea of what your income is, you need to understand how much you spend each month. What is your housing cost? What about bills you pay monthly? Do not leave out a single detail. Do you have a television subscription service that is only five dollars

a month? Include it. It will make budgeting and tracking your money a lot easier if you have everything laid out from the beginning.

3. Calculate your spending. This is the step where people get caught up. It's easy to feel overwhelmed by the task of calculating your spending, but only after doing so can you really begin to understand how to make a realistic budget. There will be things that you won't be able to account for in the beginning, but certain expenses will be similar month to month such as travel expenses, or grocery bills.

Once you have a clear understanding of your situation, you can begin implementing the changes that are necessary to help you get control of your debt once and for all.

To pay down or to save up—that is the question.

Many people who make the decision to get control of their debt begin with a damaging misconception. It is often believed that as soon as you start cutting down on spending, you should take all of your extra money and pay off your debt quicker. This can be a useful thing in some cases, but more often than not it does nothing to break you out of the cycle of debt.

Instead, your first priority should be to focus on building a small savings. It is important to have an emergency fund so that you do not have to resort to any kind of debt in the future in the event you need extra money. So, in this chapter, we will discuss some easy ways to begin building a small amount of savings to use in case of an emergency.

Creating an Emergency Fund

As we mentioned earlier, a lot of debt is started by circumstances that are beyond our control. It is not always a lack of judgment that leads to massive debt. What you can do to stop the debt cycle is to plan ahead for emergencies. As you create your savings, you will want to aim to have at least three months of living expenses. I know, this seems like a very high amount at first read. If you start saving now you will be one step closer than you were just yesterday. The key to solving your debt problem is to focus on small and actionable steps.

I am going to provide you with a list of small ways that you can begin saving for your emergency fund. Many of these won't involve changing your budget too much, and as you see the amount grow, you'll feel proud knowing you are making financial changes for the better. Here are some easy ways to start saving now:

1. Look into easy to use programs from your bank. Some banks offer savings programs that round up each purchase to the next dollar. The change difference is then

deposited into your bank account. If you are someone who exclusively uses your debit card, this is one easy way to start saving without realizing it.

2. Begin a savings challenge. A lot of people enjoy following challenges in relation to drawing, fitness, or health, but why not follow one for savings? You can do something simple such as add five dollars each week, or if you can afford it try an extreme version and double the amount you deposit each week. Make a chart for yourself and mark off as you save.

3. Save your loose change. Each time you use cash, keep your spare change and deposit it into a jar. At the end of each month gather it up and add it to your savings. If you want to save more using cash, challenge yourself to save all of your one-dollar bills, or your five-dollar bills. Over time this will add up.

4. Set up an automatic savings deposit. Set a reminder for yourself and have the savings automatically deducted from your account. If the money isn't in your checking account, you are less likely to use it.

5. Place extra funds at the end of the month into savings. As you get accustomed to budgeting and cutting down on spending you might find you have left over funds at the end of the month. Instead of applying it to your debt, apply it to your savings account.

I'm ready to break the debt cycle and start saving! How can I begin today?

If you're reading this book it is likely that you have reached the stage where you are ready to start solving your debt problem now. That is great! As you use this book follow along with our end of chapter tasks, and you'll have easy steps to guide you in solving your debt problem. If you're ready to begin here are things you can do today to help you.

1. Put your credit cards in a hiding spot. The goal is to start paying down your debt. If you continue using your credit cards you will only make the debt grow.

2. Start tracking all of your spending. There are easy to use apps that help you keep track of your spending. If you use cash, make sure to write it down on paper so you know how much you are spending. If you are using a debit card continuously add up how much you spend in each category.

3. Make a goal for yourself. How much do you want to have in savings? Start with small goals and work up from there. Does it feel overwhelming to think about saving three months' worth of expenses? Start with one month, or one week. The point is to make goals you can meet so you build confidence in yourself.

Spending Trackers and Budget Apps

There are numerous tools available to you to use to start tracking your spending, and to create a budget once you get to that step. I am going to list a few manual and technological ways for you to easily track your spending which will come in handy when it comes time to creating a realistic budget.

1. Manually in a notebook: Carry a tiny pocket notebook with you when you leave the house and keep track of what you spend your money on by handwriting it. At the end of each week, you can add the total spent to a category within your book. For example, calculate how much you spend eating out at the end of the week.

2. Mint.com is one website that tracks your spending for free by linking up with all of your various accounts. This one is perfect for those who do not enjoy shopping in

cash. It also easily categorizes things for you.

3. You Need a Budget costs about $7 a month but can be used as an app or on your computer. It links up with bank accounts as well, but also allows for manual input for those who spend using both cash and card.

4. Clarity Budget is another good option that tracks your spending and compares it to your projected income. This one is free to use and can be used online or on an app for both Android and Apple users. It also helps you create a savings and reminds you of your various subscription services.

Your homework

Now that you've put away the credit cards, started tracking all of your spending, and made a goal for yourself, you need to start getting a clear understanding of your finances. This is your homework. Follow the three steps outlined in breaking the debt cycle. Here they are again briefly to help you recall:

1. Calculate your income.
2. Write down all of your bills and necessary expenses.
3. Choose a spending tracker system that will work best for you.
4. Calculate as much of your spending as possible.

Once you do all of these, you'll be ready to start working on a clear plan to tackling your debt, increasing your savings, and raising your income.

How Much Do I Really Know?

Here is what you'll learn in this chapter:

- **What should I know about my debts?**
- **How can I keep track of my financial information?**
- **How do I find my debtors?**
- **What is the snowball or avalanche effect?**

For those of you who are moving through the book in a linear fashion, you have now come to your next big step. In the last chapter, I focused on giving you the tools to start breaking out of your debt cycle NOW. If you followed the homework, you should have a pretty clear idea by now of how much your income is, how much you pay on average in "bills" and "essentials" and hopefully you've started tracking your spending. Now that we know these things we can begin moving forward.

The next step is to figure out how much you really know about your own debts. How much is your total debt? Who do you own money to? How long will it take to pay off all your debt? What are your interest rates? These are all questions I will guide you in answering in this chapter.

Like most problems, debt is an issue that needs to be faced head on and with full knowledge. You need to know exactly where you stand, how bad your debt is, and what is costing you the most money in order to find the best way to tackle it and fix it.

What information do I need to track down?

Finding out the total amount owed will be the first part of our information scavenger hunt. You need to know exactly what the current balance is that is owed. After that you will need to research what your interest rates are, and what you pay in interest monthly. This will come in handy as you make a debt repayment plan. Having this information will help you later on when you make a plan for which bills to pay off first, or where to apply any extra funds you might have.

Without knowing our interest rates and monthly minimum payments, we cannot create a budget that allows us to live within our means and pay down our debts. Our interest rates also give us information into which debts will end up costing us much more than the others. For some people, paying down the more costly debts is the best way to begin tackling their debt.

Tracking this information down will take some hair-pulling time that will feel exhausting, but once you have the information, you don't need to spend too much time looking again. Most of the time you can manually update your balance or have a website or app keep the information safe for you.

How will I keep track of all of this?

Totaling how much you owe isn't the only step you'll need to do. There is more information you should find that will help you create a plan for paying down your debt. It might be a good idea to create a notebook, or (if you use excel) a spreadsheet to help keep all of your information in one place. There are also numerous websites and apps that vary from free to a monthly cost. If you prefer the ease and access of a website or an app, here are a few that people have found very useful.

1. Unbury.me is a free and easy to use calculator tool that helps you get an idea of your projected debt and an idea of a payoff completion time. It offers the avalanche or the snowball payoff method which we will talk about later in this chapter.

2. Mint.com Financial Goals is free to use with a Mint membership. It'll provide you with suggestions for helping pay down your debt

after you link your accounts. Mint.com is also a helpful spending tracker.

3. Debt Payoff Assistant App is also free to use. It uses the snowball method to help you pay off your debt. You can keep track of an unlimited number of debts, you can create multiple payoff plans, and you can use their calculators to help make a decision.

4. DebtTracker Pro is $1.99 a month and allows you to use any payoff method to control your debt. It's an easy to use design for those who want the ease of an app without the background of technology knowledge.

5. Undebt.it is a website that offers two options: a free membership with basic tracking, calculations, and projections, or the $12 yearly fee which gives you access to saving challenges (like the one we mentioned in the first chapter), bill management, and more.

Who do I own money to?

Tracking down some of your debts and their collectors will be fairly easy. Others might take more time. I'm going to guide you through a few different ways of finding out your debts.

1. The first place to begin is by going through your credit report. Most people don't know that you qualify for a free credit report yearly. Most banks also offer to give you your credit report. There are three major bureaus you can get a credit report from and each one allows it to be done once a year without cost. You can get them all at once, or spread them out.

    If you are beginning to gather information on your debts it might be a good idea to collect all three free reports at one time. Often, a small debt may show up in one report and not another. Begin with the credit report and you will have most of the information you need.

2. One easy place to begin is by contacting the places you do know you are in debt to. This will include all credit cards whether they are linked to banks or not, credit lines with stores, your car payments, your mortgage company and other similar accounts. You should know most of these major ones. If you don't know who owns some of these debts, proceed to the next step.

3. The next place to look is on your credit report. Most banking institutions offer free yearly credit reports. It is good to get them each year so that you can stay up to date on your credit. It is even better if you can get your report from the three major credit score companies. Sometimes one debt may be listed on one report, but not on the other.

4. If there are other debts you know are there but can't find the information easily through your credit report, consider contacting the original lender if it is a debt that went to collections.

Often times they will tell you who they sold it to and when.

5. If you have a lot of student loan debt with different institutions, the easiest way to find out exactly how much you own, your interest, and when your payments begin is by going to studentloans.gov

6. Keep in mind: There are some debts that may not be listed. Debts that have been sold too many times may come back to find you later on. Others may have been missed by credit reports.

Snowball? Avalanche? What does it all mean?

By now you have heard the phrase "snowball" or "avalanche" in reference to paying off your debt. These two words basically describe two different methods of paying down your debts. Before I begin to describe both, the important thing to know is that they both carry the same basic principle. Focus on paying down one debt at a time while maintaining the minimum on the others.

The snowball method of debt repayment is well known and can easily be described by thinking of a snowball. When a snowball begins it is small, and as you roll it down a hill it collects more snow and grows larger. The idea here is to pay the minimum amount due each month on all of your bills, and to apply any extra funds available to your smallest debt. As you pay off one debt, you gain confidence and improve your credit, the you can move on to the next smallest one.

The avalanche works in the opposite way. This one as well asks that you pay a minimum on all accounts, but instead of focusing extra funds on the smallest, you focus your funds on the largest debt and pay that off first. The idea here is that you will save more money by paying off the larger because of the larger interest.

A good balance between these two can be reached by considering the interest rates of all your debts. Which of your debts costs you the most interest each month? Sometimes smaller debts with higher interest rates can have a much larger impact than a large one with a low interest rate. This is why gathering your information is necessary.

Know your terms!

Have you ever logged on to a credit company the day your payment was due, processed a payment, and then later found you were charged a late fee? Things like this happen all the time especially to people who hold more than a couple of debts. This is why it is absolutely important to know the terms of your accounts.

Fees paid outside of what is going to your debt is just another way for you to put money in the pockets of the company. Take the time to review the terms of your debts. Here are some easy questions to ask yourself:

- At what point will you be charged a late fee?
- When does the payment need to be processed by?
- If you are mailing a payment, does it need to arrive or be postmarked by a certain date?
- Does my interest increase after a certain time period?

Finding out these details could save you a lot of grief later on.

Your Homework

Now that you have an idea of how much you really know, I am going to give you a few more tasks to complete before you move on to the next chapter. This will help give you a strong base to move forward in building a budget, creating a debt repayment plan, and improving your financial life.

1. Pick your financial tools. What are you going to use to store all of your debt information?

2. Find out who you own money to. If possible, get a credit report (or three)!

3. Calculate the necessary details: total debt, interest rates, amount spent on interest monthly, and minimum payments.

4. (Optional) Consider which option may be best for you, snowball, or avalanche. Maybe a mixture of both?

Do's and Don'ts while becoming debt free:

What you will learn in this chapter:

- **What to avoid so you don't fall back into a debt cycle.**
- **What to add to your life to increase savings and cut down on spending.**
- **How to make small changes that will positively impact your finances.**

Now that you understand fully what your financial situation is, it is time to start making active changes to your lifestyle and in the kind of financial decisions you make. This chapter is going to give you clear advice: what to do and what not to do when it comes to getting out of debt free. Much of this advice is going to be easy to follow, but it will require effort on your part. You will need to actively make the right choices, and sometimes change can be difficult for people.

If you're ready to begin making those changes, the first thing we are going to review is a list of "don't" or what you should avoid when breaking out of debt. Let's get started!

Don't ignore those bills or your debt!

If you are reading this book, you clearly are ready to face your debts head on, but this isn't a decision you can go back on. It is important that you open all of your bills the minute they arrive. If you get calls from debt collectors, answer them and find out what your options are in terms of repayment. When you ignore your bills it can bring a lot more damage whether in terms of higher interest payments, loss of cars or credit lines, lowered credit score, and the possibility of being evicted.

Don't fall behind on mortgage, rent, or car payments!

These kinds of payments allow you to have a place to live, a means of transportation to and from work or to necessary appointments. When you fall too behind on rent and mortgage, you risk losing your home to eviction. Car payments as well are likely to lead to repossession. Loaners do not care if you are only one payment behind, it can happen out of nowhere. Sometimes we fall into situations where it is impossible to make every payment that month. If this happens, reach out and do what you can to ask for extensions, but never miss your car or home payments.

Don't avoid budgeting!

Budgeting takes some extra time and energy, but with a little bit of effort, it can be an easy habit to build. When people spend without creating a budget and tracking their expenses, it is a lot easier to spend money that should be spent on bills. In addition, it is important you review your budget often (at least a few times a year) to make sure you are raising and lowering the categories that need it.

Don't let the creditors push you past your limits!

Often times, when people begin receiving multiple calls from multiple creditors, they feel inclined to make a large payment to the creditors who call them or reach out to them the most. People often think if they make large payments the creditors will stop calling them so often, but that is not the case. As you start paying off your debt, you will need to be specific about which debt receives more than the minimum payment.

Do not let the creditors push you past your limits. Make your decision based on what will bring the biggest negative effects instead. This does not mean that you avoid paying your bills. Even smaller creditors such as credit card companies, can eventually sue and gain the right to remove the debt from your paychecks.

Don't agree to terms you cannot keep!

When you begin repaying your debts, you will need to make arrangements, but it is important you only agree to terms you can keep. Follow your budget and make payments that fit within those guidelines. Do not process payments with checks when you know the money is not available in your account. If you do not have the money, do not make the payment in the hopes that the processing time will take long enough that you receive your pay.

In addition, you want the creditors to believe you will make the payments you agree to. If you start making agreements you cannot follow through with, then they will begin to doubt what you say.

Do not continue using your lines of credit!

This should be common sense, but sometimes it is important to be reminded of the common sense because we can easily talk ourselves out of it. As you start paying down your debts to various credit lines it is important you don't start using it again. This is even more important if you have used these lines of credit for cash advances as the interest rate will not go back to normal until you pay off the amount owed.

When you go out somewhere, leave your credit cards at home. Better yet, hide them away in a place that is not easily accessible. It is good to have them in case of a very clear emergency, but do not use them when you can easily just avoid the purchase all together. This is where budgeting will also come in handy. With a budget, you will manage your finances and avoid using credit cards when it is not necessary.

Do not use your home as collateral!

Oftentimes when finances are extra tight, people consider turning to loans that ask for your home as collateral. Do not do this. Like we mentioned early on, your home and your transportation are the two things that, if taken, can drastically change your life for the worse.

Do not get a loan that comes with large risks!

Building on the last subpoint, never sign up for a loan that asks for a large collateral. Anything that comes with a high risk is a very big no. These types of loans make it easy to fall into a much larger debt. If you make one mistake with these types of loans and loan companies, you could lose a home, a car, or be garnished drastically.

Now on to the list of do's!

Now that you have taken in a large list of things that you should avoid at all costs, it is important to move on to the list of "do's". What follows will be a list of changes you can make to start positively impacting your finances. These tips will help you increase your savings, pay off your debt, and improve your credit score.

Do consider asking for help.

If you have a large amount of debt and are completely unsure of where to start (even after reading this book), consider going to credit counseling. Be sure it is a nonprofit organization, however. Many of these offer financial type workshops that deal with budgeting and lifestyle changes, and they can help you create a plan for paying off your own without living off of ramen noodles.

Do be open to consolidation.

For those who have too many debts to keep track of, debt consolidation might be a good move. Getting a debt consolidation loan could mean you focus all of your efforts on one large payment instead of smaller payments. There are also balance credit cards that allow you to transfer all of your credit card debt to one card with a longer 0% interest rate promotional period. These may be good solutions for you, and it is always a good idea to be open to them.

Do cut out costs that are not absolutely necessary.

This can be a tough one for some people. There are many people who make choices that are just outside of their means. When you decide to focus on becoming debt free, you will need to make sacrifices, and this includes cutting down what is not absolutely necessary. Now, with a budget, you can include periodic treats or expenses that are not essential, but the first step is to trim spending overall. Do you need all three subscription services? How often do you go out to eat? Where in your life can you trim your spending?

You do not need to cut out absolutely everything, but consider what is most valuable to you, and where you want the extra money to go. Some people need to go out for coffee at least once a week. Don't feel guilty if that's you. But know that you cannot become debt free and maintain a lifestyle of everyday coffee, full cable service, a gym membership, and three magazine subscriptions. Pick and choose what will save you money and keep you happy.

Do save with coupons and sales!

If you are going to spend money on something, do your best to make sure the cost is as low as you can possibly make it. Each week you receive adds with lists of deals and coupons. Most people toss these aside and shop at the same one store. Sometimes spending more time going between stores can mean larger savings in the end. Try to shop for groceries when they are in season or from local sellers who can often give you a better deal.

Start using coupons. Some people are embarrassed by using coupons when they go out, or when they make a purchase, but doing so will help you reach your goals a lot faster. If you make many online purchases consider adding an extension to your browser that automatically saves you money, such as *Honey*.

Do set up auto debit when possible.

As we mentioned earlier in the book late fees can add a greater cost to your budget and bills. For those who have multiple bills due in a month, the auto debit feature may be helpful in making sure you do not miss a single payment. There are also many companies who offer free payments by doing auto debit whereas a phone payment may result in a small convenience fee. This is the best way to avoid extra fees and to keep your credit score improving.

Do be on the lookout for free resources.

How many times have you purchased a book in the last six months? How many times have you rented a movie, or worse rented a movie and got charged late fees for failing to turn it in on time? Have you signed up for language learning courses? These are all examples of things that are offered at your local library. A library membership is free! If you are truly trying to cut back on your spending, renting movies and books from the library is a great way to do it if you normally buy or rent these from other places.

Take the time to research local resources in your community. Outside of the library, there are many cities that offer things like a food pantry, free canned goods, or locally grown veggies. There are plenty of options, but it will take a moment of research to find them. The library is a great place to start because they often know of many local resources.

This also includes entertainment. Movies, amusement parks, restaurants are all great, but definitely costly. There are plenty of resources available for free entertainment. Consider visiting a museum on their "locals" day when there is free admission. Visit the local park. Find free music or entertainment events at your local library or park. Explore the natural landmarks near you. There are plenty of things to do that can be cost effective and entertaining.

Do go for used.

If you have to make a purchase, consider browsing for used options first. Clothing from consignment and thrift shops are often way more affordable. Many of these places also offer high quality items, not just no-name brands. Plus, used clothing is already perfectly broken in!

Likewise, when shopping for household items, must-buy books, electronics, etc., consider browsing for used options first. A new bookshelf can run upwards of a $100 but buying one from a consignment store or off of craigslist can save you over $50 on that same shelf.

Do learn to say no.

There will be times when people will invite you out or ask you to buy some of their essential oils. You will need to learn to say no. It's important to prioritize your financial health. Sometimes you can give a yes, but more often than not you will need to practice saying no to save your money.

Do sell what you no longer use.

Remember when we suggested buying used? There are many people who, like you, are going to be seeking out used items to save money. If you have things around the home that you no longer use, such as furniture, clothes, books, it might be a good idea to start selling them. Consignment stores are a great place for higher quality items. Consider selling old books on sites like eBay. Have other items? See if you can get rid of them on Craigslist or on Facebook marketplace. $20 for an old shelf may seem like nothing, but that is twenty dollars you can apply to your emergency fund or to your first debt!

Do meal plan.

Now is the time to tell you that if you are someone who eats out a lot, that is one big way to cut down on your expenses. One way to cut down on eating out is to focus on meal planning. There are numerous free videos and blogs that help guide you in prepping lunches for a week at a time.

Meal planning ahead of time also insures you only spend what is absolutely necessary at the grocery store. That, in combination with shopping sales and using coupons, is going to help lower your grocery bill by cutting out spontaneous or duplicate buys.

Do find affordable hobbies.

Since you will be focusing on cutting out unnecessary expenses, it is important to look at your hobbies as well. If you are trying to get out of debt, paintballing as a hobby may not be the best way to save money. If you buy up numerous sewing patterns, but rarely follow through with them, consider cutting back. There are plenty of hobbies you can find that are more affordable, such as volunteering, reading more, writing, or upcycling.

Do be honest about your financial status with loved ones.

Parents, this is especially important with children. Discussing budget and being honest about what you can and can't afford teaches children to live within their means and allows you to live a life where you don't feel the need to lie about why you can or can't do something. Instill healthy financial habits young by being upfront.

For those who are dating, it is important you let your romantic partner know that you are making choices that will supportive a healthy financial lifestyle. Even if it is early in the relationship the person should be understanding and want to help you grow and succeed. Don't be afraid to suggest affordable or free dates too! Being open allows you to live an honest life, and it will show your partner you make quality financial decisions.

Finally.

This list is by no means exhaustive. There are many things you can do and avoid to help solve your debt problem. These ideas, however, are easy to begin right away and are bound to make positive changes in your life.

Your homework

Now that we have given you a big list of do's and don'ts, it is time you start putting them into action. Here is your easy to do homework.

1. Pick 3 don'ts that you can start fixing right now. Avoiding using credit cards is a positive and easy place to start.
2. Pick 3 do's that you can begin implementing tomorrow. Are you a reader who has avoided the library? Are you an impromptu shopper who wants to start meal planning? Find what most inspires you and try it out.

3. Finally, give yourself a pat on the back! You have already made it to chapter three! You are on the right track to changing your financial life for the better.

Changing your mindset: How to embody being debt free.

What you will learn in this chapter:

- **How does a mindset influence your ability to pay off debt?**
- **What mindsets should I have?**
- **How do I change my belief systems surrounding money?**

Why do I need to change my mindset?

Paying off your debt is just as much about your relationship to money as it is about instilling healthy financial habits. If you view money as this awful and terrible thing, everything that you do in regard to money will feel punishing and terrible. You need to consider how your relationship to money might have worsened your debt.

When we focus on our mindset, it becomes easier to instill healthy habits, to make necessary changes, and to feel good about doing all of these things. It is only then that we will be able to maintain these changes for as long as we need to.

How to practice being grateful.

When you begin making lifestyle changes to better your credit and rid yourself of debt, it can be easy to feel as if you are being forced to give up things all of the things you enjoy. Some people go as far as to view it as a punishment. These changes aren't going to be easy, but it is important to try to find a way to remain grateful. You are not being punished, you are making adjustments to change your life for the better.

You might have to make many uncomfortable changes, but the changes are ultimately going to lead to a life where you are happier and are not as burdened by debt. Focusing on the things you are grateful for can help you see your changes as a positive thing. Thus, making it easier to maintain these changes.

One way to begin is by developing a gratitude practice. Grab a spare notebook and keep it by your bed. Every morning, write down one thing you are grateful for upon waking. This will teach you to start the day with a grateful mind and to make decisions from the emotion of gratitude. At the end of the night, write down a moment in the day where you felt gratitude. Learn to start and end the day with a grateful mind. When you take time to be grateful at night, you realize that many of the changes are leading you to a better place. And while some may be difficult, it isn't making your life entirely miserable. There is still a lot to be happy about.

Let envy fuel you.

This might seem like a strange mindset change, but consider the following: what do you normally do when you feel a moment of jealousy or envy? Most of the time, people easily turn to moping or feeling pity for themselves. Sometimes these feelings can come on at work when someone gets noticed. Maybe the envy comes from seeing someone else spend on something they cannot spend on. Or maybe you feel jealous when you see someone drive a nice car.

Whatever the reason for the jealously, instead of turning to pity and moping, use it as a fuel. Consider what it will take for you to get to where the other person is. If a person at work is getting more attention, why are they getting more attention? Are you working equally as hard as they are? Is there a way for you to push yourself to earn that raise? If you see someone driving your dream car, write out a ten-year plan for yourself. What steps will you need to take to get that car?

Jealousy is not always an unhealthy emotion, when we accept the feeling and try to understand it, we can use it as a fuel to make positive and necessary changes. Don't be embarrassed when the emotion arises, instead think about what you can do to be in a similar situation. Let the envy become a means for being more productive and driven.

Learn to be an opportunist.

An opportunist is someone who takes opportunities and uses them for personal gain rather than being guided only by strict principles and plans. If you are trying to save money and pay off debt, look for opportunities to do so. How might you be able to add more to your emergency savings fund? Are there chances at work to earn overtime? While others might not want to work overtime, is that an opportunity you are willing to take to improve your situation?

After following our advice of do's and don'ts, are there other opportunities in your life where you can cut back on spending? If you do not have the ability to work extra hours or an extra job, consider what other opportunities are available. It is time you focus on problem solving not inability. Figure out what things work for you and follow through with that.

Take up every opportunity you can to educate yourself further. If you have free time, learn more about money management and debt control. Spend time browsing for frugal meals. Consider what items you can reuse or upcycle in your home. Even if you cannot use your time to make money, look for opportunities around you to better your situation.

Challenge the idea that more debt can solve your problems.

Other than considering debt consolidation or a balance credit card, there should be no other consideration of taking on more debt. Many people who find themselves in debt cycles ended up there because they resorted to more debt to solve a problem. Taking on more debt temporarily will not solve your problems. This is why it is so important to start a small savings fund as soon as possible. When you have a small savings to turn to in emergencies, you will not need to take on more debt to fix your situation.

Many people view debt as a way to get things they want as well. If you are reading this book however, you have likely started this journey because the debt has clearly become a problem. Focus on the fact that you want to change this situation instead of considering how taking on more debt can get you something you want short term. Keep focusing on what you want long term.

Focus on problem solving in a way that doesn't create more debt. Are you limited in how much you can spend on transportation? Do not take on an additional "gas" credit card. Instead consider commuting or carpooling one day a week. Change how often you go out on the weekends. When you have become accustomed to turning to credit as a way to problem solve it can be easy to want to continue that patterns. But learning new habits is also easy, it only requires time and effort.

Embrace being fed-up.

Yes, I know I said to be grateful, but it is also okay to embrace being exhausted by your situation. Do not let it overwhelm you, but let it drive the decisions and changes you make. By accepting that you are unhappy with your current finances, you can finally move forward and follow the advice of this book to change for the better.

If your debt keeps you up at night, as it has done for many people, use that stress as a fuel. Stop viewing it as something that is beyond your control and start viewing it as a problem that can be overcome.

Every time you make a decision regarding your finances, turn to those stressful nights. When someone invites you out for the second time in a week, consider how you will feel after you spend that money. When you want to sign up for a gym membership, consider if the gym benefits outweigh the costs of knowing that $40 could have gone to a minimum payment. This is not a suggestion to be self-punishing, but to consider instead what you want long term and not just short term. Remembering the difficult moments when it comes time to making a decision will help you realize

`61

what you really want out of your life and not just what you think you want in a single moment.

Be responsible for your part in your life.

It is true that sometimes debt happens with no real fault of our own. Maybe the cause was a medical emergency, or no other way to pay for school. Either way, it does you no good to focus on why it is not your fault. You have to own your debt and take responsibility for it. If you continue wasting mental energy complaining about your issue, you are spending energy that could better be used on thinking of more solutions.

Realize how many others depend on you as well. For those of you who are parents or are responsible for caring for someone else financially, realize that you need to be responsible and focus on crafting goals and meeting them. You have people depending on you. If you do not have someone you are responsible for, you still have yourself. All of those things you want in life will only be achievable if you actually follow through with your financial goals and start saving.

Are there ways for you to have the life you want while also being debt free? Do you enjoy traveling? Can you find a way to earn a living in a new place by teaching or transferring your job? Are there ways you can maintain your lifestyle while spending less? If you are single and live alone, can you consider getting a roommate to lower your rental costs?

Make goals and strive to reach them.

Make it a point to set reasonable goals. When people are asked to make goals for their lives, they can often set large unreachable goals with no clear timeline, thinking it will drive them towards what they want. You have to make reasonable goals however, with a clear end date. You also need to make both short term and long-term goals.

For example, if you are reading this and thinking, "well my goal is to pay off my student loans as soon as possible" you will never reach that goal. Why? That goal has no clear deadline, and it is likely that you have a large amount of debt to pay off. You will likely only ever see that number and get overwhelmed. How can you rephrase that? Begin by setting an end date. "I want to pay off my student loan debt within five years." Great! Now you have a point to look forward to, and a timeline to work towards.

Another key is to set a short-term goal. It can be overwhelming to think we will not be happy if it takes ten years to pay off our debt. How about adding on a specific goal. "In one year, I will pay off one whole loan" or "I will pay off all of my credit cards in two years." These are all reasonable and reachable goals that will help you feel proud of the changes you are making.

Change how you view money and debt.

We have been trained to see debt as something that is normal, as a way to grow and be a successful adult. This is not entirely true. While some credit is good, as I mentioned, much of it is very damaging. You need to change how you view debt in order to change your relationship to it. Stop seeing debt as something that is acceptable as long as you can manage it. Do not take on extra debt and payments when you are doing well because you do not know if one day you might have difficulty managing it. Live within your means instead.

Start seeing every single cent as something that can help. When you begin making larger payments on your debt, do not be discouraged if some months it is only $10 extra. This amount will help lower your total amount and with each extra bit, you will find your debt will be paid off faster. Focus on the fact that you did well and have $10 more to apply to your goals! For some payments, an extra five dollars a month means you cut down your overall by six months or longer. How much then can twenty a month do?

Remember that you are not the first person to attempt to pay off your debt. That is why this book exists! There are so many other people who are in situations like yourself, or who have been in your situation and have succeeded. Take the time to read success stories. Find out what other people have done. Use it as a way to see that change is possible and you can reach your goals.

Reward yourself.

Making these changes is difficult at first! Be sure to take the time to reward yourself, and to show yourself some extra care and joy. Obviously, the goal is to continue saving money so do not go on a lavish vacation after a month of paying a little extra towards your goals but think of what you can do once a week or once a month. Can you take the night off, lounge in pajamas, and watch a movie? Can you take a bubble bath? Maybe you skip the housework one day and go to the park to read in the sun.

Give yourself a reward each time you make a goal, or each time you practice a healthy financial habit. If you collect your change, for example, and throw it in savings once a month, then maybe that night you treat yourself to an at home face mask. Find DIY self-care tips online and do the ones that bring you a moment of joy.

Focus on what you can do.

Do not allow yourself to be overwhelmed by what you cannot do and focus instead on the things you can do. Maybe you cannot pay off all of your debt right now, but you can budget and begin paying down one at a time. If you cannot work an extra job, do not punish yourself for it. Instead seek out other ways to save money. Begin to question why you jump to defeat instead of jumping to problem solving mode.

Your homework

Now that you've reached the end of chapter, you have an idea of what makes your uncomfortable regarding your own mindset. Did you scoff at the act of practicing gratitude? Did you think the "rewarding yourself" section was clearly not worth your time? Take all of your reactions and use it as fuel. Here is what I'd like you to do as your homework for this chapter:

1. Take five minutes to journal about your relationship to money. Begin with the phrase "When I think about money, I feel..." and see what comes out. Set the timer beforehand and let yourself write whatever comes to mind. At the end, read it back and see if you gain any insight into your own thinking patterns.
2. Pick the "mindset" you are most excited to begin practicing. Ask yourself how you can begin doing this now and get started.

3. Pick the "mindset" you are most hesitant to practice. Ask yourself why you do not want to live with that mindset, or how that mindset makes you feel. If you are very hesitant it is okay to start slow and focus on what you can do. But the key is understanding why you do not want to. Some people hate making goals because they are so afraid of not reaching them. If this is you, how can you begin proving your own self wrong and show that you are capable of change?

Money mistakes that easily lead to debt, and how to avoid them.

What you will learn in this chapter:

- **Money mistakes many people commonly make.**
- **Easy ways to avoid these mistakes, or wiser choices.**

Skipping payments.

As mentioned, late bills can rack up too many late payments. If you are behind on some bills, it is important that your first step be to catch up on the late payments. Do not start overpaying any other debt, if you back owe other companies. This will lead to a worsening credit score, and to money being thrown away.

In order to avoid this, consider signing up for auto debit programs. Once you create your budget and are aware you have the means to make all of your payments, set up auto debit so that the bills are automatically charged to your account on the day they are due. This will clear your mind and allow you to focus on more important matters.

Also, if you have too many bills due around the same time, consider contacting your lenders and trying to change your due date. Some places may be open to doing this one time which will help you balance your expenses versus your income more easily.

Borrowing money from people you know.

Just like I do not want you to take out more credit cards or loans, I do not want you borrowing money from people you know. If your family or friends have offered to help you in the past be grateful and let that be the last time it happens. When you turn to quick fix solutions it becomes easier to turn to these again and again instead of making the changes you need to make to succeed.

Also, while your family or friends may be supportive, everyone has their own lives to be in charge of. If you continue borrowing, you are changing how your friends and family view your financial health. If you have had difficulty paying them back, they will begin questioning their own judgement. Debt has already caused a lot of chaos in your life. Do not let it cost you more chaos by interfering with your relationships.

It is also important that you practice being reserved with lending out your own money. While you or the other person may agree to a set payback date, sometimes things change. If the person who owes can't pay back when they said they would, it could hard the lender. Or if the lender needs the money sooner, it can also hard the borrower. Treating family and friends like your personal credit card is only going to create more problems in the long run.

To avoid this money mistake, instead focus on other ways to come up with the money you need. Can you do a side gig like Uber for a quick twenty dollars? Can you consolidate your loans to have an easier to manage single payment?

Using your credit cards for casual purchases.

It can be easy to turn to a credit card for groceries when you are running low on cash. Do not do this. As we suggested earlier, put the cards away or even consider cutting them up. It will only hurt you. Instead keep to your budget. Also, credit cards tend to lead to greater spending. If you know your budget for your household goods is $50, but you see a candle for $15 extra and have it available, you are more inclined to buy it.

To avoid this mistake, stick to your budget exactly there is no need to save those last few dollars "just in case". If you turn to your credit cards often, consider diving your budget into cash and carrying only what you need for the expense you need it for. If you go to get gas, only take the $40 you allotted yourself.

Quitting your job with no plan.

Some jobs are miserable. Some do not allow you to pursue your passions. That does not mean you can just up and quit your job with no clear plan. You are now focusing on paying off your debt, if you leave your steady source of income in the hopes of making a greater income you will only add an even greater pressure to yourself than what is necessary.

If you want to leave your job, consider growing your savings first. Then begin looking for work while you are still at your current job. If you want to start a business, begin small and start using tools to make a step by step plan.

Signing up for too many never-ending payments.

How many subscription services do you currently have? Do you have Hulu, Netflix, Amazon

Prime, HBO Go, and Audible? Yes, subscription services can be much more cost effective than turning to cable, but at some point having too many of them leads to spending almost the same as you would on cable. Unless your job is requiring you to watch television on all services, having too many is an easy way to wind up wasting money.

Aside from entertainment, consider what other endless services you have signed up. Do you have a radio or music subscription service? Do you have a gym or spa membership? What about magazine subscriptions. I am by no means saying you need to cancel every single one of them. But to avoid this mistake look at your budget and consider how much you can and can't afford. Then go from there.

Continuing to work long term for a company with no room for growth.

Just like it is not beneficial to quit your company suddenly, it is also not a good idea to stay with a company that gives you little to no opportunities for growth. Your employer should be a place where you feel like you have the opportunity to earn more and grow as an employee. If your company frequently prefers to hire from outside the company, or they only give out raises every ten years or more, consider taking the time to find a company where your work ethic will be better appreciated. I am not saying to quit suddenly but look into other options. Is there a place where you might be given more chances to grow and make a better wage? Why not try for it while you are still employed. There is nothing to lose by trying.

Choosing to purchase a new car or leasing a car.

This is one of the most common money mistakes. Buying a new car means you will be making a large payment for many years, especially if you do not buy it with a large down payment. While you might have a stable income now, things can change suddenly. If you are unable to make a car payment, you risk losing your car and all of the money you invested into it. If you need to borrow money to purchase a car, then it is not a wise time to buy a new car.

Also, leasing a car is one of the worst things you can do. When you make payments to lease a car, you wind up paying towards something you will not own. While the payments are more affordable than buying a car, and the car is new, it is also not your car. If you miss a payment you lose the car. If you damage the car, you pay more for it than you originally signed up for. Leasing is even riskier than buying new. The best option in both cases is to buy used and to buy what you can afford now.

Choosing to live somewhere that is out of your budget.

It is a common mistake for people to sign up for a mortgage that is out of their price range or to rent an apartment that is too high. When you move into a new home, really consider how well you can afford your payment. If you are paying 50% or are struggling to get by just to live in a nice home or area, then that could set you up to fail in the future or to have difficulty making other payments.

In addition, if you are a single person, it might be a good idea to consider sharing a home with someone else. Sharing a two-bedroom apartment is often more affordable than paying for a single bedroom or a studio. If you can rent a room in a home, you might even be able to save a lot more. These kinds of options are more readily available in larger cities where the rent costs are even greater. Housing costs is one way people easily throw money away by not making the best choices early on.

Using your savings to pay down your debt.

Yes, the goal is to pay down debt. But the most important goal is to educate yourself on healthy financial habits. And using your savings to pay down your debt is one easy to make money mistake. Having savings helps prevent you from taking on more debt due to emergency situations that you cannot predict. You should especially not do this if you are considering taking money from your retirement account. Borrowing from retirement almost always comes with a heavy fee. In addition, you lose the option to gain money from compounding. While it sometimes needs to be done, it is best to avoid it. If you do choose to borrow from your retirement funds you need to immediately get to work on paying the funds back to yourself. To avoid this mistake, begin planning immediately for emergencies by starting a 3-month savings where your goal is to save up to three months of expenses.

Not sticking to your budget, or spending outside your means.

A budget it not a suggestion for what you should spend and on what. It is a set of guidelines that you must stick to. If you save a little in one category you should not then think it is okay to spend the money elsewhere. The goal is to put that extra into savings or towards debt. Now that you have made the choice to get out of debt, it is imperative that you avoid spending excessively at all costs. This means spending in all categories as well. If you are someone who likes to go out for drinks, each beer or wine could add up over the course of the night.

While it might feel embarrassing to have people be aware that you are not spending as much as they might be, it needs to be more important to you that you avoid spending what you do not have. To avoid this easy to make money mistake, consider taking cash with you when you leave the house. Take only what you are okay to spend, not a cent more. If you have a card you are a lot more likely to use it.

Avoiding financial plans or setting goals.

Without a clear goal or plan, it becomes easy to push aside the need to change your financial habits. Avoiding setting a goal is really just avoiding reality. The truth is that you need to change your money spending and saving habits now if you want to get out of debt sooner than later. Consider adding some time into your weekly schedule to review your financial plans each week. Continuously update and check your budget to avoid overspending, and to help you meet savings goals.

Forgoing insurance by choice.

There are times when people cannot qualify for public health assistance insurance, or they have lost their job and their insurance. This is not a moment where I am trying to blame them. What I do consider a big money mistake, however, is choosing to forgo insurance. If you are trying to cut down on savings there are a lot more places where you should look first than by cutting your insurance premium.

Choosing not to have insurance can lead you to spending a lot more money down the line on emergency room costs, medication costs, not to mention how your health will suffer by not having access to preventative care. Avoid this money mistake. Don't cut out your insurance. This also goes for car insurance. If something happens to your car, having insurance will make it easier to continue having transportation.

Not budgeting for entertainment or fun.

The goal of making a budget is to be realistic and to have guidelines to follow. People who begin budgeting for the first time, often make the mistake of not including entertainment or fun in their budget. They assume they will cut back on all frivolous spending and never waste a cent on entertainment. All this does is lead to failure. We are human. We like to have a good time, and we have a right to have a good time regardless of our financial situation. But it is important to be wise about how you have a good time.

When you make your budget leave a space for "fun" or "entertainment" this is where you can include money for a movie ticket, bath bombs, tv subscriptions, a new accessory. Just make sure to keep the budget reasonable. I also recommend, if you must go out to eat for work lunch or while in school, be sure to include an "eating out" budget. If you only go out periodically, you can likely include it in your "fun" budget.

Buying new items to replace items that aren't broken.

Just because there is a mega black Friday sale does not mean you absolutely need a new TV. If you have a lamp that works, but is a little flimsy, you likely do not need to rush to buy one now. Buying new items when the old one works fine is one easy to make money mistake. Holding on to what you already have will help you save money.

This also applies to more than just electronics, however. If you are considering getting a new set of glasses, but the old ones work, ask yourself why you need the new ones. Are you thinking of getting a new backpack or purse? Do the old ones still hold what it needs to hold? Then you should wait on it.

To avoid this money mistake, make a goal for the new item you want. When you pay off one debt, you can begin saving towards the new item by setting aside small increments. This will also help you realize what you truly want versus what you might only want for now.

Your Homework:

Now that you've gone through a hefty list of money mistakes many people commonly make, it is time to look at your habits. Keep in mind that this list is by no means exhaustive, it is just a list of ones I most commonly see people make. So, here is your homework before you move on to the next chapter:

1. Ask yourself if you make any of these money mistakes.
2. If you do, write out a goal on a post-it note for yourself that outlines how you will fix or

change this money mistake. For example, if you frequently use your credit cards after making your payment, what can you do to avoid making this mistake? Place the post it in your financial notebook or somewhere where you can easily see it.

3. Double check your budget and make sure you have a "fun" category, and that you are not signed up for too many subscriptions.

Eight Simple Steps to Becoming Debt Free

What you will learn this chapter:

- The most important steps in becoming debt free.
- The difference in repayment plans.
- Why you either need to spend less or earn more.
- Important elements to maintaining your momentum.

Now that you have actively assessed your current state, learned all about do's and don'ts and money mistakes, and started tracking your spending, it's time to get into the main steps to becoming debt free. I will guide you through each step and help you get your debt under control.

1. Set up a budget

Thus far I have mentioned a budget many times. Now is the time to actually set up your budget. If you've been following the advice of this book you have most definitely been tracking your spending. Hopefully this, paired with the amount of your payments, means you can finally get to the step of setting up or expanding your budget.

Many people struggle with the mindset surrounding a budget. They feel budgets are limiting, like a financial diet, but that is not the case. A budget is a helpful tool that will help you manage your money and save you from drowning in debt. Once you set up a budget be sure to keep it up to date monthly. You can do this as an app, an excel spreadsheet, a google doc, or tradition pencil in a notebook

A. Start by including your monthly income as the first category, or row.

B. If you are doing this without an app or website start setting up categories for your budget on the left. Include things like utilities, rent, groceries, household, and things like entertainment, clothes, etc. Start with most important to least important. This is important as well if you are using an app.

To the right you will have a "budget" column, and an "actual" column to know if you stayed within your means. In addition to these other categories, it would be best to include the "emergency fund" and "debt repayment" categories. This will allow you to know how much you can actually put towards your debt, and how much you can focus on adding to your three-month emergency savings fund.

C. As you write each category and create the budget for the category, remove that from your monthly income. Then you will see the number go down, and you will know when you need to adjust. You can't change your minimum payments due, but you can change how much you spend on clothes or going out.

D. Finally, look at your surplus amount. Hopefully there will be a surplus amount, if not then you are still okay so long as you have included the "debt repayment" and "emergency fund" category.

If you did not have enough to include those, then consider cutting back in other places and focusing on the emergency fund. If you can't pay extra on your debt right now, read on, I will give you advice on how to make a little bit of extra money to put towards your debt in later chapters.

If you are struggling with deciding how much to allocate to specific categories look to your spending for the past month and see if you can decide how much you might need, or how much you can cut back on. Some financial professionals recommend following the 50, 30, 20 idea. Fifty percent of your income on essentials, thirty percent on wants, and twenty percent on savings and debt repayment. This is always a good place to start.

2. Decide on a debt repayment plan.

As I mentioned earlier, I said I would explain some of the commonly known debt repayment plans which are the snowball method and the avalanche method. I will also make a few suggestions after to explain how to create your own custom plan if neither seems fit for you.

The Snowball repayment plan focuses on the idea of a snowball. As a snowball rolls down a hill it gathers more snow and momentum, growing in size. The snowball repayment effect focuses on paying off smaller debts first and then working up from there. It is beneficial because you feel successful after paying off smaller debts, and you begin to pay less in interest over time.

The focus is on the overall amount of debt, not on the amount of interest or minimum payments. This allows you to continue momentum and not get discouraged. This is beneficial especially for those with many smaller debts.

The avalanche payment method works the opposite way. Just like an avalanche, it mimics the idea that as you pay off your most costing debts they will rolls down like an avalanche. It has some benefits such as saving you more on interest and getting the hardest debts out of the way.

In this case, the focus is not just on the largest debt, but on the ones with the worst interest rate. This is how it saves you the most money. This is a good option for those who feel secure in their ability to repay their debt, who don't need the "momentum" of the snowball effect, or who have various interest rates on their loans with some being very high.

Creating a custom repayment plan is also an option. Some people choose to combine both the snowball and the avalanche method. You can prioritize loans that are most important to you. For example, if owning your car is more important that saving on interest, you can choose to pay off your car loan first. Some people choose to repay credit cards first so they can have that as an absolute worst-case scenario backup option. Others still might focus on smallest debts with worst interest rates. The possibilities are endless. For those who just need clear direction, begin with the snowball method and work your way up.

3. Spend less money or make more money.

Later in this book we will discuss some simple ways to make a little bit of extra cash, and we have already discussed some easy ways to save a little bit of money here and there. The main third step however, to becoming debt free is recognizing that you need to focus your extra energy on one or the other. Living the way you have been living has contributed to your debt or worsened it if the debt was out of your control.

You cannot expect to have different results by living the same way you have been living. You will need to make a decision whether you will drastically reduce your spending, or whether you will try to take on additional ways to make an income. If you are someone who has up until this moment lived a pretty carefree lifestyle with large expenses, then maybe cutting back on spending could drastically help you pay off your debt quicker. If you have been living relatively within your means, then perhaps a smaller side gig might be more beneficial to you.

If you decide to cut back on your expenses drastically consider these two biggest expenses: living and transportation. Are you set on living the way you have been living? If you are a homeowner with a mortgage, might it actually be more beneficial to rent instead of own? Renting often comes with built in maintenance, stable utilities, and no surprise construction costs. If you have been renting but living alone, might a roommate scenario help you save?

For those who feel their income covers the basics, but want to do a little bit more, read on. We will share some tips for making extra cash. Also consider a part-time side gig that can be strictly used to pay down debt.

4. Negotiate!

Many companies don't want you to know this, but they want to keep you happy, and making payments. When you begin repaying your debt, it is important to take the time to contact your creditors. While it may take a few hours of hold time, you might be able to get a lowered interest rate or talk down the amount in a payoff estimate. A slight decrease in interest won't cost the company too much, but it will make a difference in your payoff timeline.

Likewise, it is important to try to do this with other kinds of expenses. Can you talk to your cable provider? What about getting an income-based rate on some utilities? There are countless ways to try to reduce the overall amount spent in different areas simply by taking the time to ask.

5. Consider other options.

For those who don't feel as if they can add on a part-time job, or if a part-time job feels like it won't do much with the amount of spending that is required of you, consider other financing options. There are 0% balance credit cards that allow you to pay as much as possible in the first year. By transferring all of your credit card debt to one card, you will only need to navigate one payment and can work towards trying to reduce your overall credit card debt.

This is a great option especially for those with multiple cards. If you are paying even $30 interest on 5 cards, that is $150 that is going just to interest each month. A balance transfer credit card will allow you to use that $150 and more each month to lower the overall amount due without accruing more interest.

There are also consolidation loans, which we have mentioned. It becomes much easier to pay off your debt when you only have one payment you need to make, and one debt you can apply excess income to, versus multiple accounts. If you knew you had $10 extra one week, adding that $10 to the one debt account is much more manageable than trying to decide which of your 5 payments to apply it to.

For those who have good credit, consider a personal loan. Personal loans often have a fixed repayment term meaning you know when the full amount will be paid off and how much the payment is each month. They also tend to have a lower interest rate than a lot of credit cards. You can then apply the personal loan to your worst debts. Do not however, sign up for a personal loan that uses your home or car as collateral, or that asks you to pay an exuberant interest rate if you miss a payment or go beyond a certain time limit.

6. Use cash as much as possible.

As mentioned earlier, cash is a good way to stop yourself from overspending. But beyond that, it is easy to organize, divide, and save. If you take your paycheck, cash it, and then divide the cash for your necessary expenses you will not be tempted to borrow from one category to add more to another category.

Many people use an envelope system, wherein they assign each spending category an envelope and place the money in the envelope. When it comes time to spend from that category, they take out from that envelope only. It is a good visual and tactile way to keep yourself on target with your budget.

7. Use extra cash, windfall money, and paid off debt payment amounts toward your debt.

Anytime you get a work bonus, or get extra cash whether birthday money, cash rewards, or tax returns, you should be applying that towards your debt repayment plan. This might mean you apply it straight to payments or to creating an emergency fund, either way it should be helping you avoid and/or reduce debt.

As you continue paying down debt, you will eventually reach a point where you won't have to make payments anymore on some lines of credit. Do not readjust your spending. If you have been living with your budget for a while, give yourself a small reward, and then use that money and apply it to the next debt. In this way, the more you succeed, the more you move towards less and less overall debt.

8. Reward yourself.

Obviously do not go outside of your means, but if you are continuously setting and meeting goals then you should be incorporating some type of reward system for yourself. There is no way you will continue paying off your debt if you feel unmotivated to do so.

Some easy ways to motivate and reward yourself are by giving yourself a day or night off. Stay in, cook a pizza in the oven, and watch a movie. Don't focus on your finances or your side gig, just enjoy a day without the idea of debt in your head. Maybe your reward is to make yourself a couple of margaritas at home. Think of the things you enjoy doing but don't always get to do because of budget, try to find a way to make it DIY and do it at home so you don't have guilt from overspending, but also don't feel as if you are missing out.

Your homework:

1. **Spend less or make more?** Before you begin learning about more money-making ideas in the later chapters, decide if you want to focus on spending less or making more money.

Ideally, we can all do a little bit of both, but usually there is a clear direction from the beginning.

2. **Avalanche, Snowball, or custom?** Ask yourself which plan will work best for you and write it out on paper. If you are doing the snowball method, where will you begin? What amount can you apply towards your debt repayment?

3. **Are other options an option for you?** If you have never looked into consolidation loans, or balance transfer cards your homework is to do more research. Compare your debts and consider whether you would benefit from one of these options. These are great for those who may be able to make large extra payments, especially the first year. Since balance credit cards often come with a year of free interest, this could be a viable option.

Money saving tricks everyone can follow

What you will learn in this chapter:

- **Easy swaps you can make to save money.**
- **Some ways to lower your expenses without doing more than a few phone calls.**
- **How to be energetically efficient and save money doing it.**

Now that I have guided you through the essential steps in becoming debt free and cutting out those bad financial habits, I'm going to push you further by giving you tips and tricks to save money, make money, and boost your debt repayment timeline forward. Below are some easy money saving tricks everyone can follow to help decrease your spending and increase your savings.

Create a pause period for any larger purchases.

The largest benefit to waiting 24 – 48 hours before making a larger purchase is the way it forces you to decide whether you really want or need the item in question. In waiting 24-48 hours before buying something, you will also weigh the pros and the cons more carefully. I don't think you should never make any large purchases just because you are trying to pay off debt, I believe the goal should always be to change your financial habits for the better. So, if you really want or need an item just consider how necessary it is now, and whether it is a great deal or not.

Try DIY Gifting

One of the biggest times each year for consumerism is the winter holidays and romantic holidays. This is a time when people feel forced to buy gifts for their friends, their children's coaches, their bosses, and on and on. Each small $10 to $20 gift can add up to a lot at the end of the season. When gift giving, definitely stick to a moderate budget. One way to do that is to try DIY gifting. With resources like Pinterest and YouTube you are sure to find ways to create inexpensive but meaningful gifts.

Consider this as well for birthdays and other holidays. How much money do you spend yearly on greeting cards for example? Why not try a watercolor tutorial and handmake a card? DIY gifts are not only frugal, most of the time they are a lot more sentimental.

Have fun nights at home instead of going out.

One of the biggest expenses especially when it comes to entertainment is the cost of going out. Each beer or wine can add up over the night. Appetizers are costly even when split between four, and movie nights at a theatre can cost $20 - $30 easily between popcorn and the show. I am not saying cut these out entirely, rather, make it a point to spend one to two nights a month in.

With so many resources like Meetup, you have the opportunity to set up fun board game nights, write-ins, movie nights, and so much more. It's a great way to save money, and to make sure you are spending quality time with the people you enjoy.

Repair items instead of buying new ones.

This is especially useful for clothes. Most people toss out jeans or shirts as soon as they have a hole in it, or a button missing. Most of these fix-it tasks are easy to do and can be learned through a picture tutorial or an online video. Embroidery, for example, is a great way to fix small holes and add a unique touch to your clothing.

As we mentioned earlier, your library is a great resource. Many libraries now offer a "repair clinic" where you can take specific type of items in with you and have professionals help you repair them. There are also numerous resources online for easy repairs.

Be energetically resourceful.

Turn the water off while you brush your teeth. Flip the light switches off in rooms when you are not using them. Turn the thermostat up. These are all suggestions that help you be more resourceful, but also will help you save money.

While cutting back on electricity might only seem like $10 or $20 here and there, it adds up over the year and ultimately means you will have more money to go towards other things. It is also a good way to make sure you are doing your part to help the environment.

Another easy to do change is to switch your lightbulbs. Go for CFL or LED lightbulbs. They are a little bit more expensive upfront but will ultimately last longer and bring down your energy cost. You shouldn't run out and replace every single bulb at the same time, but maybe choose to do one at a time and focus in the areas where you use light the most often.

You should also focus on replacing your air filters both in your car and in your air conditioning. Replacing the filters often will help keep your air conditioners running smoothly and efficiently.

Another investment might be to purchase a smart strip. When you turn off one device that is plugged into a smart strip, the other devices are automatically turned off as well. This is especially useful for work areas with desktop computers, or entertainment centers where more than one item is plugged in.

Compare prices or ask for price matching.

Instead of grocery shopping at the closest grocery store to you, consider browsing the ads and seeing which stores have the best deal. Know ahead of time what you have to buy and what you frequently buy. Go to the stores that have your most frequently bought items at a lower cost. If you have to drive a little further but end up slashing your bill by 25% then it is worth the time and gas.

Take the time to also research about price matching. Many stores will price match items that are on sale at other stores. This applies not just to grocery stores but other stores as well. While it is not always openly advertised, an online search will usually turn up answers or you can simply call and ask.

DIY what you can.

This doesn't just apply to gift giving. Look at what you most frequently buy and see if there is a way for you to cut down on costs by making it on your own. Baking bread, for example, is one thing people find they can make easily once a week and they usually save on costs by buying bulk ingredients. Nut butters are another option, along with vegetable stock. There are countless ways to DIY in your kitchen and to save some money while doing so as well.

Switch to generic items and buy in bulk.

Most people don't know that generic items are usually the exact same ingredients but at a lower cost. This is especially true for medicine, toilet paper, and canned goods. The list goes on. Generic items are usually produced by the store themselves or a manufacturer that makes multiple goods so you get a better deal because you aren't paying for the marketing budget that comes along with brand name items.

Also, consider buying bulk for some of your regular purchases. Toilet paper from a warehouse style store tends to average a lot less than most grocery retailers per unit. Most of the time when you buy bulk, you only need to make that same purchase a few times a year versus monthly. This does not only apply to household goods however, you can also buy rice, flour, oil, sugar, and other frequently used items in bulk. Buying bulk is also beneficial to the environment.

Shop around for different insurance companies.

If you are not locked into your insurance company with a contract, it is a good idea to make some calls and to gather some quotes. Some companies have great deals for new time customers. Other companies offer great benefits to college students, veterans, or educators. Simply by switching your car or home insurance you could wind up saving a few hundred dollars a year.

It is also wise to consider the level of coverage you have. More coverage is sometimes essential given the value of your home and goods, or the state of your car, but often times you might be paying more for a type of coverage that is not going to save you much in the event of an accident or other incident. Remove coverage that doesn't seem absolutely necessary or beneficial to you. Do not be persuaded into buying what the insurance company recommends just because they recommend it. They also have sales goals to meet.

Look at spending in terms of number of hours worked.

When you are considering making a purchase, think of how many hours you will have to work to pay that off instead of considering the cost. Sure, getting a great new television may be only $200 right now, but if you make $15 an hour that is over 15 hours you will have to work once you consider taxes. When you think of it that way, it changes your perspective and helps you consider just how much you want the item.

Another thought process some people have is considering the cost of an item as cash. If someone offers you $50 or the DVD series you want to buy, which are you going to take? In most cases you will be happier to have the cash and apply it to a debt or bill.

Pay your savings and debt repayment budget first.

When it comes time to divide your monthly or bi-weekly income, it is a good money saving idea to first take out what you need for savings and debt repayment. When you do this, you can then adjust your budget from there. If you try to adjust the entire budget first, you will likely allocate more money to other categories than you would for the debt repayment or savings.

Of course pay off your transportation and housing costs first, but if paying these categories causes you to lose a little bit of fun money or you are forced to cut back on groceries, you might actually be happier with the results of doing that than taking longer to pay down debt or save your emergency fund.

Consider other ways to go green.

Going vegetarian for example. Meat is usually one of the higher costs when it comes to grocery bills. If you cut back your meat consumption by only half of what it is now, you are likely to slash your grocery bill down by a drastic amount. While some vegan items may be more costly, things such as vegetables and fruits tend to run less per pound than meat.

Look at some of your smaller spending habits in terms of annual spending.

If, for example, you have a habit of getting popcorn every time you go to the movies. And let's say you go to the movies twice a month, then that adds up to about $25 dollars a month. This, times twelve months, leads to $300 which can be an extra chunk that can be applied to a debt. This also goes for vending machine spending, snacks from the gas station, etc.

Slash your grocery bill.

I am not saying to decrease the amount you consume in general; I am only saying to be wise with where you allocate your grocery money. If you find you are someone who shops without a list, and grabs what they crave, then you might be spending a lot more than you need to be. Always meal plan before shopping and avoid things like soda, cookies, and chips that do not add much nutritional value but easily eat up your budget. If you do want to buy some periodically, this is a good moment to practice buying generic.

Also, be smart about the food you do plan to make. Things like grains: rice, quinoa, and barley go far in meal planning. Rice is one food you can use to make a variety of bowls or main courses. Barley can be used to make veggie burgers as well. Beans are another great buy. They last a while once cooked, and you can make large batches. You can also easily make bean burritos to put in the freezer for when you don't feel like cooking. Consider other bulk and affordable items you can buy that will add nutritional benefit while also reducing your cost.

Consider all the vices you can quit.

Do you have a pretty hefty soda habit? Can you cut down on this? It's not a nutritional necessity and might not even be helping you feel all that great. This also goes for alcohol consumption. A few drinks periodically is fine, but if you have a rather large budget for alcohol, it might be a good idea to consider cutting back. Smoking cigarettes or vapes is another big culprit of financial drain. If you can't make yourself quit for health reasons, consider quitting for financial reasons.

Your Homework

As you can see by the list above, there are many ways to save money and even more available to you through research. These are all ones that will easily and quickly save you money, especially in the long run (one year from now and beyond). Some of these take only a few minutes while others will require more time and planning but will prove helpful overall.

Your homework is as follows.

1. Pick one money saving method you have considered but have not tried and actually try it out. See if it works for you. Have you considered going bulk, but didn't have the space to do it? Maybe see if you can find an

area in your house to store toilet paper or paper towels. This is one easy place to start.

2. Try a DIY! Are you running low on window cleaner? Look up a DIY cleaner you can make with affordable ingredients. Or were you going to run out and buy a new sweater because of a hole in your current one? Can you stitch or patch it up easily?

You're doing great so far! Read on for more ways to master your spending habits and to bring in more income!

Ten secrets the wealthy don't want you to know.

What you'll learn in this chapter:

- **Simple habits the wealthy do to stay wealthy.**
- **How to make your money work for you.**
- **How does time influence finances?**

We've all heard a tale or two about a celebrity or a wealthy individual who lost all of their finances through risky choices or improper investment selections. If you think about the number of stories you have heard, however, and compare it to the number of stories you have heard about celebrities who built an empire for themselves, you'll find that the number tends to skew more towards success than lack of it. That is because the wealthy, from a young age, understand what choices they must make to create a lifetime of healthy finances for themselves.

The wealthy do occasionally earn their stability through sheer luck, but a lot of the times they are able to continue being wealthy even after retirement because they have made choices that set them up for long term success and wealth, not just for what will make them feel greatest now. This chapter will focus entirely on the habits of the wealthy, but specifically ten habits they hold that allow them to maintain their wealth.

You yourself might not be wealthy, and might not be trying to maintain a set amount of wealth, but with these habits you will see just how much your day to day schedule and free time can influence how much income you bring in, how much money you save, and how you stay out of debt.

1. They are lifetime learners.

Every skill you gain will ultimately influence your finances in some way even if it is only slightly. Did you know that learning a new language, for example, can help you get a small raise? Most people don't know this. Some small skills that may seem like hobbies can also save you money. If you knit to give your hands some movement, or because it's an affordable hobby, you can use this to make gifts for others, or even make goods to sell at craft fairs later on.

Learning allows us to grow and change, and the older we get the more conscious we need to be about trying to actively learn. The wealthy are constantly learning new trades and tricks. Not only that, they also use every opportunity they can to look at life as a journey in learning. Instead of seeing moments as failures they look at moments as opportunities to learn and grow. This is the right mindset to have when moving forward in your debt recovery journey.

If you are interested in learning a new hobby or skill begin by visiting your local library. They often have free resources like language learning software. Many local craft or home improvement retail stores offer free weekly events to learn things like growing your own herbs or quilting.

2. They make finances a family responsibility.

There are many people who struggle to communicate with family, friends, or loved ones about finances. The wealthy, however, discuss it as a family responsibility. It is important to have your family be up to date on your financial status even if it is children. Teaching children young about financial health can benefit them as they move through life later on as adults.

It's also important to be truthful about budgets and what you can actually afford. This is true in dating, marriage, and parenting. Pretending you are doing better than you are will only lead to more debt and will eventually cause you to let someone down because they have a different expectation of what you can and can't do. Honesty is a good policy to have when it comes to money, especially if you want to continue tackling your debt.

If you have children, consider involving them in budget talks each week. Teach them about your budget and how that affects them. You can even go so far as to have them help you plan out snack purchases or entertainment for the family. If you are in a relationship, take some time to create a list of alternatives to spending for date nights. Pinterest has a plethora of "date night in" and "staycation" resources.

3. They are intentional about their focus.

The wealthy know, as many of us do, that time equals money. They often choose to focus their attention and energy in a purposeful way. This is a good habit to adopt. When you have time that is not dedicated to work or financial planning, what do you do with it? Are you purposeful about your time?

It might be a good habit to track your time for one week. Try to see where you spend the bulk of your time. Are you watching two hours of television nightly? Do you find you scroll your social media for more than an hour a day? Or maybe you see positive habits like a high amount of time reading. Tracking your time will give you insight into your own daily habits.

Consider all the ways you spend your time and see if there are changes you want to make to grow, learn, or just make yourself more joyful. Is there something you have been wanting to learn but have not made the effort to do so? What can you change about your schedule to fit it in? Sometimes it's as easy as listening to an audiobook on your daily commute. The point is to consider how you spend your time and whether it aligns with your goals in life.

4. They know to invest sooner than later.

Aside from your emergency fund, as you pay down your debt, it would be a good idea to look for a quality retirement fund and savings account. The wealthy understand the value of interest when it comes to saving money. Depending on the quality of the account, you could be saving whole payments at the end of each year in just the interest alone. If the money is going to just your retirement, or your children's education, let the money make money for you. Put it into a good account.

The sooner you can begin building your retirement the better. The wealthy often know to take advantage of employer perks like retirement matching. Do what you can to give future you a boost of extra cash. These types of bonuses are one easy way to build income for later.

In addition, consider quality investments. If you choose to begin investing, start small. The wealthy understand it does not take much to begin investing. Apps and companies like Stash and Acorn make it easy to choose portfolio packages that are low risk and meant for long term investing. They also often offer bonuses in terms of financial wellness articles and advice. Stash only cost $1 a month, and Acorn works by collecting your change from purchases and investing it.

5. They make smart insurance choices.

Earlier we talked about avoiding paying too much for insurance coverage you do not need. But it is also important that you have the insurance coverage that will most benefit and help you. If you have a high value car for example, then it would be a good idea to improve your insurance coverage. Or if you have an electronic device you use for work that can be costly, and you rent a home, then renter's insurance might be best for you.

Be sure to make the right choices in regard to health care so that you have proper preventative care without many out of pocket expenses. A higher premium might save you more in the long run in terms of emergency room or urgent care costs. Life insurance is also one area where you do not want to go too low. Be sure you put your family's health, safety, and wellbeing first and foremost.

Also look into your insurance selections and see if there are some tax-free spending options. Some companies offer flexible spending accounts that take money out from your paycheck pre-tax and deposit it into a spending account for medical purchases. This is a good way to budget for any medication, vitamins, or alternative health options you regularly pay for, while also saving on how much tax you pay.

6. They surround themselves with people who will help them reach their goals.

The wealthy are, as noted, wise about their time. This includes who they spend their energy and resources with. Be sure that you surround yourself with people who are helping you achieve your goals. If your friends are constantly pressuring you into making choices that aren't good for your financial healthy, then they are not helping you be the best you can be.

People offer invaluable information and knowledge in your lives. They help you grow as a person. The people around you should be a source of comfort, but they should also push you to be a better version of yourself. Consider attending social meetings for people who are looking to learn a new skill, or meetings such as Toastmasters that allow you to meet new people and learn something.

Who are the people you spend the most time with? How have their habits started influencing you? Most people don't notice these answers until they take the time to think about it. Even if it is a work colleague who only wants to go out to happy hour, and doesn't seem so happy about their work, could their small talk be affecting your own sense of gratitude or work ethic?

You don't have to completely cut out the friendship, just learn to recognize the behaviors and mindsets you want and don't want when it comes to your friendships.

7. They prioritize work when it comes time to working.

One of the key traits of proper time management is making sure you work when you should be working, and you "play" when it comes time to play. The wealthy understand that it is important to prioritize work above relaxation and play most of the time. This doesn't mean they do not enjoy themselves; I am sure they do. But they know that they need to make the most of each day and try to accomplish more than they did the previous day.

There are plenty of resources for time management. Some people focus on doing tasks and work in blocks. Spending only a set time on each task and then taking a small break. Some people prioritize easy to complete tasks over harder ones so they can get more done in a day. Consider how your own time management skills affect you.

When it comes time to work, focus your energy in that area. Then you won't feel guilty when it comes time to unwind and relax later on. This does not only apply to your career, but also what else you do with your time. Don't scroll through your phone when you are supposed to be managing your finances. Focus on the task at hand and let the other things be their own time slot in your day.

8. They understand the value of income, not just salary.

The wealthy make smart money choices that allow them to make the most income with the least amount of work. It is not just about making money by doing your 9 to 5 job, you also have to find ways to try to increase your passive income. One way is by finding a quality savings account, another is by making smart investment choices. It is also important to find a career that will provide a greater income to you in the long run. Choose a company that offers great retirement benefits, or room for growth.

For those who want to start a business one day or who have skills they want to try to turn into an income, begin researching ways to make a passive income. Can you start a blog? Do you have a knack for graphic design and illustration? See if there are ways you can take what you already do and make extra income from it.

The key is to understand that your time is also your money. If you can make income that does not require active work time, then you are prioritizing your skills and adding more to your in-flow of cash.

9. They write things out.

The wealthy understand that nothing is an actual goal until it is written out with a date on it. This includes your financial plans as well. You cannot expect to stick to a repayment plan, a budget, a savings plan, without first writing it out. Make it a point to make contracts to yourself and to follow through with them. If it helps, write it out and place it somewhere you can see it every day. Doing this with smaller goals will be especially helpful as you will be reminded to make daily choices that help you grow towards these goals not away from them.

This is also beneficial for your daily tasks and schedules. The most productive and wealthy individuals track how they spend their time and how they prioritize tasks daily. Starting with to-do lists is the easiest way. Write out what needs to get done and number them from most to least important. This will help you focus your energy and time more efficiently.

This is also why I have included many brief question answer type homework assignments. I want you to see your own goals and ideas in paper and to think about them as you move through the book. Writing things out forces you to also put your ideas into words. It's not just about thinking of what you want, but also considering how you will get it.

10. They focus on their thinking and mindset.

This is precisely why I have a whole chapter on mindset and changing your thinking regarding your finances. The wealthy live in a world of surplus and not scarcity. They make choices that help them remain in a state of surplus, not choices that are influenced out of fear. When you make choices from a positive mindset, especially about your finances, you are able to change how you approach saving and spending your money. You make choices that bring you joy in the long run.

This is also why it is important to reward yourself and to practice gratitude. You cannot succeed if you don't recognize your own successes.

Your homework:

1. Let's start with the write it out tip. Write out one short term financial goal. It can relate to savings or to paying off debt. One good place to start is by saving $1000.

2. Look at your own time management skills. Are you prioritizing your passions over things that are simply eating away at your time? What change can you make today to start making better use of your time?

3. Consider your relationships. Do you surround yourself with people who want to help you grow? If you don't feel like your friends understand you, where can you go to meet people who are on the same growth paths as you?

How to start budgeting like a pro

What you will learn in this chapter:

- **What is most important in creating a budget?**
- **What are the various methods to budgeting?**
- **What do I need to know for my budget?**
- **What mistakes should I avoid when budgeting?**

Earlier, in chapter six, I gave you a bare bones way of creating a budget. But budgeting requires practicing conscious effort, and a set of skills that also require practice. It is difficult to jump into budgeting if you have spent your whole life either avoiding a budget or working with one that was overly simple. That is why this chapter is going to focus on the essential aspects of a budget, and how to do it in a way that is most beneficial for tackling debt.

Many of these tips will work for everyone, but some might not feel fully suited for you. If that is the case, take what most helps you succeed, and leave out the rest. Before you make the decision not to do something, however, consider at least trying it. Many people are hesitant to make changes because they fear the change. Ask yourself why you are hesitant to make a certain change, and then decide if it's fear of the uncomfortable talking, or if it is truly not meant for you.

Don't let fear drive the choices you make in regard to budgeting and do not let comfort stand in the way of your success.

1. Choose your method of budgeting.

This is essentially what you will be using both to track your spending, to allocate your funds to categories, and to create your budget. There are plenty of free resources, but the options will fall mostly into the following categories:

1. Pencil and paper: The traditional way of budgeting. This is good for those who are interested in the envelope cash system. Also beneficial for those who are more tactile in their processing. Basically, this involves the same aspects as a spreadsheet but not on a computer.

2. Spreadsheets: These can be done through google sheets and excel. There are many pre created sheets available for free download online. If your career requires you to be skilled in excel or sheets, you might prefer this as a blend between the modern aspects of an app or website, and the traditional aspect of pencil and paper.

3. Websites: There are countless websites available that help you create and stick to a budget. Many of them are also free. Websites are a god tool for those who use cash and prefer to update their finances once a week or at most once a day. They are usually easy to navigate,

especially given that you can do so from a computer. They are more modern than a spreadsheet, but less time intensive than an app.

4. Apps: There are so many apps available for tracking spending and budgeting. I have already listed a few in earlier chapters that I find useful. An app is useful for those who like convenience and are looking to build strict habits. With an app, you are forced to update as you spend and as you move through the day. This is also useful for those who don't prefer using cash and would rather budget for a debit card.

2. Decide on your preferred budgeting system.

Not all budgets are created equally. You will need to decide what type of budgeting system works best for you. I've highlighted some of the most common ones along with their key traits to help you decide what will be best for you.

- The traditional list, or line-item budget: This is the classic, but more time-consuming budget. It requires creating categories for everything, deducting as you spend, and it requires you use every dollar. This is a very detailed process and requires knowing exactly what categories your spending falls in to. It's time-consuming, but it works very well. For those who need to cut back on spending drastically, this could be for you.

- The envelope system: If paying for everything with cash appeals to you, then this might be your system. You assign each category of spending an envelope. Come payday, you take out what you need for each budget and you place it in its appropriate envelope. When you run out of cash, you run out of the budget. It's great for those who need to physically find a way to limit their spending, or for anyone who might be more of a visual learner, if your envelop is empty you are unlikely to try to spend more money.

- The fractional budget: This is the budget process that we mentioned earlier wherein you spend 50% of your income on your necessary expenses or needs, 30% on your wants, and 20% toward debt and savings. This is beneficial for people who don't like the nature of line budgets. The fractional budget is a good one for those who are new to budgeting and who have a steady income that does not fluctuate too much.

This is also good for those who are not sure how to begin allocating funds. For those who have high necessary expenses each month, this might not be as ideal. You can, however, also try to change some of these percentages. Say doing 60% needs, 20% wants, and 20% savings and debt. It is helpful when trying to instill a debt repayment habit.

- The Zero-Sum budget plan is good for those who have a flexible income or who are usually left over with extra funds at the end of the month and are unsure of where to apply it. The main focus is making sure every dollar of your income has a purpose. If you have leftover money then you apply it to debt repayment, savings, or you increase the amount you apply towards other necessary expenses.

3. Know your net income and your will-go's.

Your net income, unless you work as a freelancer or other individual with a flexible income, should be the same approximately each month give or take some overtime. It is essential you know this amount, or at least a safe estimate before you begin your budget.

Once you know how much you make each month you can begin divvying up your dollars to the appropriate categories. Keep in mind, when it comes to categories you can go as specific or broad as you need to in order to help you succeed. For those who are more advanced in their budgeting skills, it might be time to start going specific.

Regardless of your skill level when it comes to budgeting there are some "will-go's" that are essential to know and include in your budget. Housing and transportation (or the essential/needs for those doing fractional) is the most important. These categories should include your mortgage or rent, your insurance related to living (medical and home), your car payment or related transportation costs, and any taxes associated with either of these.

Once you know these numbers you can move to your next more urgent costs. This will likely include your other debts such as student loan payments, credit card payments, and utilities. You will need to make at the very least the minimum payment on all of these to continue to build your credit and get out of debt.

From there we can move on to the "other" category which could include childcare, other types of debt repayment, grocery costs, basically anything that is practically essential or which you would suffer if you defaulted on. The final category is focused on debt repayment and building savings. From there, it is up to you how you split your categories.

Prioritizing your categories in this way can help you see where you *need* to be spending your money so that you don't suffer further debt consequences. In addition, it can help you discover just how much you are spending on needs and if there is an area you'd like to try to reduce your costs.

4. Write out three versions of the same budget.

Now that you have started crafting your budget, it's a good idea to write out three versions of the same budget. I know, that sounds like overkill, but hear me out. When you begin budgeting, or get serious about budgeting, you usually have a budget that you are "going to try very hard to stick to" and this is your "flawless" budget. It's the budget you want to stick to because it will save you the most money and get you out of debt the quickest.

The problem with the flawless budget is that it is just that, flawless. It isn't a real budget and it doesn't take into accounts that you are making changes in your life and that sometimes the changes come with difficulty. This is where budget number two comes in: the "reality" budget. This is the budget you have been living with. So, fill in the same budget bit with all of the money you have been spending thus far. Write it out, even if some of the numbers freak you out.

The third budget is the happy, "middle-ground" budget. This is the budget that will take into consideration how you have been spending, and what you would ideally like to spend. As you compare those two extremes you can begin finding a number that will lead towards active change, while still considering that you don't wish to live off ramen noodles for a year.

When you have both budgets in front of you, you can begin making changes that will help you have more money to pay down debts. It is about making choices that will change your life for the better, not trying to live a lifestyle you simply won't be able to sustain.

5. **Reassess your budget often**

As you learn how to budget and work on building your budgeting habits, you will want to check in with the budget at least a few times a year. Early on, once a month would be better. Budgets change as do needs and income, so you'll want to figure out what helps you be successful the most as your life changes around you.

A good idea to keep this habit going is to set up a routine financial date with yourself. Some people prefer to do it after they make an important payment like rent or mortgage. That way, money is already on your mind and you know you will be assessing your budget at least monthly.

6. Tips to continue being successful with your budget

First, it's a good idea to share your budget with someone who is close to you and who wants you to succeed, for some your partner might be your spouse or significant other, for others it might be a close friend who is also trying to get out of debt. Whatever the reason, find someone who is just as committed as you are. That way you can ask them for feedback when needed, and you can check in with them as well.

Second, this type of budget is set up for standard daily living, but there are numerous of expenses that will not fall into this category. Take birthdays, weddings, holidays, for example, these are all cases when you might need to spend more money than you would like to. It is important to begin a separate budget for these as the time nears. If you know you spend a few hundred each year during the winter holidays, then you might need to start budgeting in the summer before.

A budget is not a financial diet, it is a way of living so that you give yourself the best options for success. This means you need to plan ahead and make wise choices.

7. **Why some budgets fail, and how to avoid it.**

There are many of you who are likely very new to budgeting, but I am sure there are some of you who have tried budgeting in the past and felt like they failed for whatever reason. I am going to go over some of the smaller, easy to make mistakes, that often impact how successful we are with budgeting.

Mistake number one: People fail to account for some expenses. There are certain expenses that come a few times a year, ones such as car repairs, or start of the year school supplies, or annual-type payments.

Many of these are costs that we know are coming at some point, but we fail to plan far enough ahead for them. It is important to consider all of these costs when writing your budget. It is easier to set aside twenty dollars a month towards future tires, than it is to buy them new out of one month's income.

Mistake number two: Many people who are new to budgeting try to create an overly complex budget that ultimately makes it too difficult to track, update, and follow. If you are new, go easy on yourself and focus your energy instead on small habits that will lead to greater successes. Account for what is most important in your life, but don't think your budget needs to look like everyone else's budget. The key to a budget is to make it your own.

Mistake number three: People don't stick to it or follow it long enough to see if it works. This is especially true once someone feels like they have made a mistake. Let me make this very clear, even as you budget you will make a mistake. It is okay! It is normal! If you make a mistake do not give up, and do not think you are hopeless. It is important that you continue bettering your financial health. Getting out of debt is more likely when you implement small and helpful changes. It is less likely to happen if you focus on making a giant change without being able to follow through.

Your Homework

I know this chapter was a lot of information to take in, especially if you are newer to budgeting. Now that you have learned ways to either further develop your budget, or to begin one from scratch, I have some necessary homework for you. This will be good to do before you move on to the final chapters, as this chapter is probably one of the most important ones in the book.

1. I am going to lead you through creating your three versions of your budget. First, begin with the dream version. What you would like to

ideally be allocating to each category in order to maximize debt repayment and savings. From there, create your actual budget, then start recreating the budget with the mindset of "balance". This should be the budget you aim for each month.

2. Pick a day of the month that works best for you to sit down and check in with your budget. Make a date out of it, grab your favorite, use the paper you like, grab colorful pens if it helps. Whatever will make you follow through—use it. Then follow it up with a mini reward even if it's an hour of trash television. Remember, it is important to reward yourself.

3. Finally, and this is the most important assignment, actually begin budgeting. Start following through. Don't be afraid of making mistakes, don't push the start date later because you want to make some bad spending decisions. Start today. There is no better day than today.

How to Master Your Spending Habits

What you will learn in this chapter:

- **Easy choices to make to have control over your spending.**
- **Ways to avoid overspending.**
- **Places to check your budget for unwise spending.**

As you learned in the last chapter, having a budget is not the only thing that will help you achieve financial success and break out of debt. You need to actively implement the budget in order to be successful. Not only that, but you need to change your spending habits for the better. This chapter will be entirely focused on helping you master your spending habits so that you can more easily follow your budget.

Many of these tips will range in theme whether they deal with mentality like discussed in the earlier chapter, or simply making wise money choices. While it might feel like an exhaustive and overwhelming list at first glance, many of these stem from simply asking yourself questions before you shop. Only you can make the necessary changes needed to master your spending.

Find your purpose!

Decide why it is that you are making these changes and what you want to achieve. If you have your reason and purpose in mind as you make daily spending choices, you can then remind yourself what the end goal is. Now that you have a budget, use this reason as a way to boost your own ability to succeed.

Know the why of all your purchases!

If you are considering buying something, you should always know the "why" for your purchase. There are many times that people make a purchase simply thinking they need to, or it's about time they do so without having a true reason. This is especially true for people updating their phones, televisions, or cars. Why are you buying the latest version? Is your current television not working? Is your car more trouble than it's worth to maintain? If the answer is yes than you might have a solid reason to make the purchase.

If you find that you cannot think of a good reason to justify many of your purchases, then perhaps it is a good idea to wait it out. Maybe you can go another month, or another year with the product you currently have. The more use you can get out of your item the greater the value and the better your dollars were put to use.

Research before you make your purchases!

Always do your best to find the most affordable price even when it comes to something as small as groceries. There are numerous stores that price match simply by showing an ad online on your phone, or bringing in the competitor's ad. Also, if you see a sale price in an ad, be sure to take it to the store with you in the even there's an error in the cost displayed.

Sign up for weekly email newsletters with coupons. Research for available coupon codes online before making a purchase. Likewise, make smart choices about whether to buy new, used, or refurbished. If you need to purchase a new television, a refurbished one is a great choice for example, and it often comes with a warranty so you know you'll have one for at least a year.

This is also important for very large purchases such as a car. Many people worry that a used car won't last as long, they fear the history of the car, but a used car can be a great way to save money. If you research and buy from a reliable seller than you have no need to fear. The worry comes in when you focus too much on a deal and then lose reliability as a result. A well cared for used car will always be a better purchase than a new car that needs to be financed in terms of bettering your financial history.

Add in fun funds!

You are trying to make changes for the better so that you live your life in a new way. This isn't, as we said earlier, a money diet. You should be allowed to have fun when it comes to spending. Just be wise about, set aside a small frequent amount or a larger periodic amount that you save up over time.

By adding in "fun" money, you are less likely to make an impromptu mistake. Without allocating any fun money, we tend to make spontaneous choices to throw out the budget "just for one day" but that can be more harmful than actively planning for fun. Decide what kind of fun is most important to you and take the steps to add that into your life.

Double check your monthly expenses as a yearly cost!

When you are creating your budget, or updating your budget, it might be a good idea to turn your monthly cost into a yearly cost. This is especially helpful for "smaller costs" that might add up easily over time. A coffee at $5 a day, five days a week, is only $25 a month. This might not seem like a great cost considering it helps boost productivity, but when you consider that it is actually $100 a month, or worse yet, $1,200 a year, then the cost might actually seem too high to be worth it. Consider it also in terms of hourly. Do you make $25 an hour? That means one hour of your work week will automatically go to coffee. You do not need to cut it down entirely, but just scale it back to avoid the overall high yearly cost.

Create your own retirement nest egg and don't rely solely on public benefits.

Many people avoid planning for their retirement because they assume they will work longer than they will, or they think social security benefits will be enough to cover their living expenses. This is usually not the case. It is important to begin planning for your retirement as soon as possible. While you might think it has nothing to do with being money wise or paying off debt, it actually does.

When you pay into your retirement account, a lot of the time you do so pre-tax, so your actual earned income is reduced before taxes are taken out. This is a way of saving dollars easily. Also, if your employer offers a matching benefit to your retirement then you could be saving double what you are putting in just by using the program. This is one of things the wealthy know to take advantage of.

Putting money into your retirement savings is a way to make a small, extra, passive income. You build your savings by doing nothing but letting it sit in the account. Of course, paying back owed debt is important, but it is also possible to start depositing small amounts into your retirement account from each check before you budget out the rest of it, even if it is only a few dollars.

Plan as best as you can for the future and for big changes.

Sometimes debt happens because of happy lifestyle changes. Maybe you have just gotten married and decided to start a family suddenly but found that when the baby arrived you needed to take loans out to cover one or more of the missing incomes. The truth is, there are many unexpected joys in life, but as someone who is choosing to become financially wise, it is urgent that you take all the necessary steps towards planning for these futures well ahead of time.

If you know you will be marrying in a year or two, for example, do not settle for a loan to cover all of the expenses. Instead make the smart choice to begin setting aside money early. Decide what you can DIY for the wedding, or where you are willing to save on spending. I can guarantee you a marriage will begin with much less stress if you avoid signing on for that extra loan so early on.

Take care of your expensive, or more costly, items!

Don't avoid getting an oil change just because it comes with a cost you don't want to pay. Take care of your car at the times it needs to be taken care of. In the end you will find that caring for your car saved you a lot of grief and money in the long run. An oil change could be under $50, but needing to buy a new car, or fix the engine after you avoided getting the oil change can lead to hundreds if not thousands of dollars.

This also goes for other costly items. Take care of your computer. Routinely delete unnecessary files, clean it, clear up temporary memory, take it to a specialist, do what you can to make sure you don't need to make another large purchase any time soon.

On the flip side of this, do not sign up for unnecessary warranties just because it sounds as if you will be taking better care of your products. Dealer warranties for example that come with oil changes covered are often more expensive than paying for the oil change. Especially if you find a local coupon.

Most products already come with a manufacturer's warranty, so adding on an extra warranty isn't entirely necessary or useful. In some cases, it may be helpful, but ask yourself if it is entirely necessary before you tack it on to your costs.

Find the places where you are unnecessarily spending double!

Do you have a gym where you live that is free, but still pay for your gym membership? Do you have an e-book or audiobook membership, but also a library account? There are numerous times where we are paying double for something we don't need to be paying double on. Take the time to analyze your monthly costs to see if there is anywhere you can easily cut out some of this double spending. If you pay for cable and subscription services, for example, you are throwing money down the drain.

Early on we provided you with a list of resources to browse when trying to reduce your spending, use this list to see if you can find any places where you are spending unnecessary cash on things you can easily access for free.

Learn to avoid places that make you want to spend excessively.

Some people might not be able to resist buying a new journal, or a new tee from their favorite store. If there are places that actively lead you to spending more money, then do your best to avoid going there unless necessary. Don't try to spend an afternoon at the mall "for fun" just "window shopping" if all it does it lead you to making purchases that later lead to guilt.

The same goes for online shops. If you have a place that you frequently like buying new merchandise from but you know they are not needs and are not within your budget, then don't browse. Avoid doing this as a distraction as well. Do not browse recommended "must buy lists" if you know you have an issue avoiding making impulse purchases from your favorite store.

While this may sound like it only applies to buying items, this also applies to going places where you know you will spend money in general that you do not have to spend. If you live near a casino, do not go with friends there just to throw away money you could be using elsewhere. Don't go out for drinks where the happy hour makes you want to buy more than one or two items.

Avoid overspending just because you have the "funds".

It can be easy to make the choice to spend more than you originally budgeted for when you have extra funds available either in another budget category, or on a credit card. This is a big mistake because it causes you to avoid actually sticking to your budget. When you are forced to use only a certain amount you begin making wiser choices and only choosing to spend on what is most important to you.

But if you decide to use an extra $10 on your credit card to cover that fancy mustard you have been eyeing, you're not letting yourself have the opportunity to develop the habits you need in order to get out of debt.

Set specific goals!

As we mentioned earlier, it is important to set a date for your goals, but it is also important to make sure your goals themselves are specific. You need to have both a short term and a long-term goal with "due dates". Otherwise you will not have anything you are actively working towards.

One example of a good long-term goal is to pay off all of your credit card debts within five years. Or to save for a deposit on a home within ten years. The key is to know approximately how many years you want to spend trying to reach that goal.

More important than long term goals, however, are short term goals. They are the goals that will help you align and develop towards your long-term goals. One short term goal could be to save up $1,000 in emergency fund money within six months. Another could be to save for a vacation within a year. Whatever the goal is, it needs to be within the one to two-year mark, and it should be something that is fully achievable. Also, it should help you grow towards your overall long-term goals.

Be wise with your food related expenses.

For starters, really look at your eating out expenses. Most people find they are spending way too much in this category. If you buy lunch every day of a five-day work week, even if it's only a $5 sandwich, that adds up to $25 a week, which adds up to $100 a month, or $1,200 a year! And that is if you are eating pretty cheap. Instead buy what you need for an easy lunch and meal plan. This will automatically help you gain control of your spending.

Next, take a look at your grocery budget. There are some things that cost more, meat products for example are one. Now, I am not advocating for you to go wholly vegan but consider if you can skip out on meat for one dinner once or twice a week. This will instantly shave some dollars off of your grocery budget.

Don't be afraid to buy store brand or what is affordable. Some organic produce is a smart move but focus mainly on the dirty dozen if you do shop organic. Buy the rest when it is in season or on sale. Farmer's markets often offer good prices on in-season produce. Try to make your own grocery items. Some people save vegetable bits and make their own broth which can easily be frozen.

There's no need to drastically change your diet and resort to eating the same foods over and over but do take the time to look at your expenses within this category and see if there is anything that can be reduced or cut back.

Read all of your contracts all the way through!

For those of you considering helpful tools like balance credit cards, anyone making a repayment plan with a creditor, or anyone on the verge of signing a new contract, take the time to actually read and browse all the way through. There are often tools that can be helpful down the road, or there might be stipulations you had not considered.

Balance pay-off credit cards are great, for example, but you usually need to pay off the debt within a certain amount of time otherwise you pay exuberant fees and absurd interest rates, at which point the credit card only harmed you more than it actually helped you.

Get in the habit of reading any and all contracts that ask for a signature.

Avoid following trends.

Since we live in the age of social media, it can be easy to feel as if you are missing out by not doing the latest and greatest hobby or having the most up to date telephone. Make it a point to question your purchases. Are you simply following a trend or are you making a purchase that truly makes you happy?

Much of social media and trends is orchestrated to increase sales. This is not uncommon knowledge. So, make it a point to check in with yourself to find out if you are buying something simply because you believe it will lead to happiness.

The latest "self-care" trend is one example of this. Many companies are using the term to boost their sales, comparing buying their produces to acts of self-love, but this is not always the case. Sure, buying something you need and want can be an act of self-care, but more often than not self-care looks like other things such as taking care of your finances, taking care of your physical and mental health, or giving yourself rest and water when you need it.

Your homework:

This chapter was focused on all the ways you can gain control of your spending and avoid making the errors that might have led to your debt in the first place. Now that you have a great set of tips, it is time to move on to your homework assignment for this chapter.

1. Double check your food related category on your budget, or your most recent food expenses. Was there an area where you could potentially save a little bit of money? Are you someone who has a habit that needs to be acknowledged and broken, such as going out for lunch daily? What can you do to change this today? Write out the steps and follow through with it.

2. Make a list of all the places that are likely to lead to overspending for you. Once you acknowledge your financial weakness, you can begin taking the steps needed to avoid those places or only going with a set budget. Is it a place you *need* to visit often, near work for example? Can you consider only carrying cash when you are nearby? What can you do to set yourself up for success?

3. Recalculate some of your smaller monthly costs as annual costs. How does it make you feel? Are you happy with the amount you are spending yearly in certain categories? Are you happy with the number of hours it will take to cover those yearly costs? If the costs still don't seem like much to you, then good job, you have found a compromise in your budget. But if the amount makes you cringe, then maybe it's time to reassess that small area.

Ways to Increase Your Income

What you will learn in this chapter:

- **Small ways to boost your income from home.**
- **Possible ways to make money in your free time locally.**
- **Income avenues for those with unique skills.**

I mentioned early on that there were two ways to solve your debt problem: one was to decrease and correct your spending habits, and the other was to increase your income. This book clearly focuses on changing your spending habits and decreasing your spending. But I did want to take the space of the final chapter to give you some helpful tools to increase your income.

Clearly, the more income you can make the more likely you are to be able to save more money and to repay debts more quickly. So below you will find some ways that you may be able to make more money.

These are not meant to replace full-time income streams. Rather, they are meant to be ways to boost your influx of cash periodically. Try out the ones that appeal to you and fit your lifestyle, but don't feel the need to do every single one of these all of the time.

Try out the gig economy and drive for Uber, Lyft, or Door Dash!

This is an obvious go-to for people who have their own cars with insurance. The nice thing about these jobs is that the hours are completely up to you. If you are someone who stays up pretty late, and you live in a city with an active night life, then you might be able to work 2-3 nights a month and bring in an extra payment towards your debt easily. You'll want to do your best to earn positive reviews by being courteous and a good driver. The better reviews you have the more likely you are to attract more passengers.

Some time frames and some areas may not be a great option for this side gig, but it's worth giving it a shot especially if you have a well maintained car with great mileage.

Fill out some paid surveys while unwinding at home!

Paid surveys are not going to bring in a great deal of money but doing a few each night might add up to an extra boost for your savings at the end of the month. Many of them take only a few minutes to do and can be done with only half of your attention, while the rest of it is focused on the latest television drama.

Swagbucks is one popular go-to for many people. This site even offers extra pay for doing things like watching short videos. Companies understand the value of surveys and having people share their opinions so they're willing to pay a small cost (small to them) to get your views. Survey Junkie and Inbox

Dollars are two other companies that are often listed as popular options for surveys.

Sell what you no longer need or use!

There are so many options for selling used items online. Not too long ago it felt like the only way we could sell used goods was to do a garage sale or to list items on craigslist. Now there is Etsy for vintage goods, eBay and Amazon for used books and other goods, ThredUp for used clothes. The options are endless, the key is to find the right place for your items. Even if you only make a few dollars, taking the time to make the listings is usually an easy process and can add up quickly.

Most people don't know that they can also sell things that no longer work. This is especially true for electronics as many people will buy things up for parts. Even old, broken down cars can bring in a few hundred dollars.

Rent out your home or a spare bedroom!

Do you have family you can stay in for a few days at a time during the summer? Do you live in a popular tourist spot? Do you have a spare room you wouldn't mind letting people crash in? It might be a good idea to consider opening up your home to an Airbnb guest. Some seasons and places can bring in a good deal of extra income. Beach cities are one prime example of this, as are major metropolitan areas.

More and more people are choosing to stay in privately owned homes than opting for a hotel because it cuts down on costs and gives them the feeling of a home away from their own home. This business can be especially lucrative if you are willing to rent out your whole home. If the process seems daunting, consider finding a vacation rental management company to oversee it. They might take a small cut, but they will handle all the financial and business aspects of the rentals.

Play video games and stream them!

Does playing video games help you unwind? If you play them often you could make a nice extra bonus each month simply by streaming your video games and sharing them online. There is the potential to make money by having visitors view ads, sometimes people sponsor you, and some viewers even donate money to their favorite channels.

Twitch is one website that allows you to try to make a revenue by streaming your video game use. You earn money through views and sponsorship and could wind up making thousands of dollars on the hour. This is great if you have a video personality and already play video games often.

Post YouTube tutorials, unboxings, reviews, etc!

YouTube is one way that you can bring in passive income. You have the potential to make thousands of dollars for every million views. All you need to do is decide on a focus, begin recording and post it. Once the video is online it starts gathering views. Sometimes the funds don't come in right away, but they will add up over time.

Many people find success with tutorials, especially when it comes to things like art, makeup, crafts, or cooking. While the YouTube pay is nice, oftentimes you can also earn free products in exchange for videos. If you enjoy having an online presence or sharing videos of things you are passionate about, this might be a good option for you.

Make some extra bucks losing weight!

This is only if you are already in the process of losing weight in a healthy way. There are numerous websites dedicated to making a "bet" on yourself. You usually pay a small fee upfront to be put into the "pot". If you lose a certain amount within a certain timeframe you split the pot with everyone who lost the money.

Some bets can be done on your own or with a group of other online individuals. Some can be as little as twenty pounds spread out over six months or as quick as 4% loss in the span of four weeks. The websites encourage healthy weight loss. It can be a great way to find support for your weight loss goals and make a little money betting on yourself. Healthy Wage and Diet Bets are two of the go-to sites available online now.

Use rebate type apps!

This is another example of getting cash back on purchases you already have to make. Ibotta is one example of a place that credits you back money for your grocery purchases. All you need is a receipt and to scan the items they ask for. By doing this you get a small credit deposited into your account within only a few days.

Consider doing some freelance work!

There are plenty of websites, like Fivrr, for example, that allow you to offer your services for a small fee. This is a good way to gain a small amount of extra income especially for those who have highly sought-after skills like graphic design, SEO skills, and marketing. If you have a skill you'd like to offer for a reasonable site, consider looking up other freelance websites.

This is especially good if you have some extra hours each week to devote to this work. It's all done from home and can be done on your own schedule. Do you have any skills you could offer such as proofreading, or editing?

Ask for a raise!

There are some companies that have built in raises, but there are many who don't have a set schedule for when they increase pay. If you have been with your company for some time or have started taking on more work than you used to do, or are doing better work, then it might be time to consider asking your boss for a raise.

It can be a difficult conversation to have since many people are not accustomed to asking for a pay rate they actually deserve, but this is your sign to take the leap and just ask. Be prepared with a list of reasons why you deserve the raise. More often than not, if a company wants to keep you and keep you happy, they will give you at least a small increase.

Work as an assistant, whether virtual or locally!

Websites like task rabbit are set up for people to seek out someone to finish tasks they can't personally accomplish. Often, they will be things like grocery shopping, building furniture, mailing items, and other simple things that can take a lot of time or be difficult for people who have disabilities or health issues.

If you have a flexible number of daytime hours available and you have an interest in accomplishing small tasks in your local area, then TaskRabbit might be a good boost of income for you. Most of the time the task will take less than an hour but can make $25 to $50 just to ship out some packages. There are many tasks available such as mounting a television, cleaning a part of the home, or planting flowers.

There are also many part-time gigs available for virtual assistants. When some people make a good deal of money as lawyers or doctors, some minor tasks like making appointments or responding to emails, could take up some of the time they could be using to make more money. In that case it is easier to hire someone to do the minor mundane task for them. If you are good at research, clerical skills, or good at making phone calls, you might be fit for a virtual assistant gig.

Consider teaching!

Aside from YouTube, there are also many websites that give you the option to make money simply by teaching a course on something you love. You can try to do this through a website such as

Skillshare or do this as a webinar or class on your own personal website. This is especially useful for skills that people have a deep interest in like hand lettering, watercolor, cooking, and other similar hobbies and skills. Some Skillshare teachers make thousands of extra dollars from classes they made years ago.

In addition to online opportunities, you might be able to offer a local workshop. There are plenty of locations where you might be able to host a workshop either for a fee or by donation. If you have a skill set people are interested in learning you could boost your income simply by teaching a course in a day or a weekend.

Use your knowledge on specific topics to make money by answering questions!

There are plenty of websites that allow you to collect money for answering questions about specific trades or a skillset others don't really have. Websites like Just Answer make this easy, but there are also other websites like Enotes, give you a chance to put your degree to use to help other students struggling to understand their course materials. Most of the time each answer has the potential to earn you a few extra dollars just by sharing skills you already have.

Turn your hobbies into cash!

People absolutely love handmade and vintage goods. If you enjoy doing DIY projects or updating old furniture, then you could make a great deal of money. Just like people flip homes for a profit, you can flip thrift store goods for extra income.

Sometimes all you need to do is repaint an old dresser and you could sell the same dresser for twice what you paid for it. This also goes for clothing. If you know how to add personal touches to vintage clothing, then you could resell the items at a craft fair or online through sites like Etsy.

Turn your social media into a money-making venture!

For those of you who are active on social media, a lot of the time you can earn free goods or make money simply by using your reach to boost sales for other companies. While this might not make you money overnight, you can easily start moving toward this venture by reviewing and sharing things you already love.

If you don't wish to use your personal account to try to promote other companies, you can use your skillset to apply to virtual part-time social media management jobs. Places like Freelance have many jobs like this or offer the opportunity to make a few dollars by sharing your views online. Some people have made thousands of dollars through sponsored tweets for example!

Your homework:

Now that I have shown you a plethora of income boosting opportunities available to you, it is time for you to do your final chapter homework assignment! There are many opportunities on this list ranging from time consuming too easy to do small tasks. Here is your homework:

1. Pick out one income boosting activity that you know you could easily do and take the steps to do it. If this is signing up to fill out surveys, then sign up now! What is stopping you? There are bound to be a few minutes each day where you could be making some extra money.

2. Consider if there is a skill you can offer. Do you have a degree in marketing, and can you handle doing some social media tasks? Do you know how to make crafts and have an interest in doing YouTube tutorials?

Find the thing that is unique to you and try to turn it into a passive income.

Conclusion

Congratulations! You have finished the entirety of the *Debt Free Masterplan.* If you have followed along closely, and completed the homework, then you have taken the necessary steps towards building a new life for yourself. You are on the right path to reaching success, getting out of debt, and changing your habits for the better.

The goal of this conclusion is just to remind you of some of the most important elements of this book. Once we go through those, I will give you your final homework assignment, and hopefully you will walk away with a new set of tools and a new mindset towards making the changes you most wish to make.

Chapter one focused on breaking out of the debt cycle and saving money as soon as possible. The most important takeaway here is that you need to do all you can to avoid going further into debt. Stop any of the unhealthy habits you have in regard to spending whether this means cutting up your credit card or avoiding payday loans.

In addition, you need to start saving money immediately in the event an emergency arises. Medical issues, car issues, and loss of job are some of the biggest contributors to debt, but with a small emergency savings fund much of it can be stopped before the debt gets bigger.

Chapter two asked you to find out as much information as you could about your debt. At the end of this chapter you should be more aware of what you know and don't know. The key is to consistently have a place to record this information and to update as needed. If you don't know your debt information chances are you took on debt without really reading the fine print or knowing what you were getting in to. Now you can avoid this in the future and make your changes with all of the information at hand.

Chapter three taught you all about debt through a series of do's and don'ts. The key here is to avoid the do nots whenever possible, and to begin making changes to include more of the do's than you currently do. Becoming debt free is all about making small daily choices that lead you closer to your goal. Chapter three gave you a list of things to begin implementing immediately so that you can save money quicker and avoid spending so much.

Chapter four was helpful by reminding you how important it is to analyze your own mindset regarding finances and spending. It stressed the importance of gratitude and implementing a gratitude practice. From a place of gratitude, you have the power to make choices that will drive you closer to your goal through happy choices not a place of suffering and sacrifice.

In chapter five you learned some of the most common money mistakes people make and how they easily contribute to debt. Be sure to recall the advice we gave to avoid these errors and to stay on the right path. There's also some great advice on what to do to avoid falling back into the debt cycle.

Chapter six was focused on getting out of debt and the essential steps you will need to follow. We discussed everything from budgeting, to savings, to using cash as often as possible. Budgeting and cutting back on spending are two essential traits to getting out of debt, but there are also other choices that can help you get on the right path, like negotiating, or going 100% cash. The key to this chapter was to continuously check in with all of the larger steps needed to becoming debt free. Don't expect the budget to do all the work for you.

As we moved into chapter seven, I tried to guide you in how to be wise with your money by making smart saving choices. This was a lengthy list that focused on different ways you could potentially up your savings by small, but focused choices. Some are easy changes; some might take more time. The key is to continue trying them out before deciding they aren't for you.

Similar to the mindset chapter, chapter eight was all about the wealthy and what choices they make in their lives to continue growing their finances. In this chapter I gave you the secret tips the wealthy don't like to give away. The focus for this chapter was on finding ways to increase your income without increasing your time spent such as choosing the right savings account and retiring early.

Chapter nine was a step by step guide to setting up your own budget. This is an essential skill you will continue building as you move through your life. The chapter focused on trying to find what was right for you whether that was a paper budget or an app, whether it was excessively detailed or just detailed enough. There is a budget style for everyone out there, the key is to try out a few different things and then pick what you like. I also urged you to consider writing out three different versions of your budget so you could balance the dream version with the reality version for a budget that is created through compromise.

Chapter ten built on all you have learned and taught you how to make smart money moves. This chapter focused on Choices you have to make often in order to save money or make the most of your money. There are important reminders like "check your food expenses" and "avoid trends" that most people don't realize can contribute to debt or at the very least, unwise spending.

Finally, chapter eleven was a sort of "bonus chapter". We know that debt repayment is done through cutting back on spending and by increasing your income. Much of the book focused on cutting your spending, but this final chapter gave you a list of ways to boost your income in small ways. Hopefully, there was an idea on there you could not wait to try out.

We know that getting debt free seems like an impossible task, but after reading this book, hopefully you have realized that it is an entirely reachable dream. Not only that, but it can be done just by making small everyday changes. In addition, it is important to remember that you are making changes for your lifestyle not just temporarily. You will need to take the time to continuously check in with yourself to see if you are doing all you can to be your most successful self.

Your final homework

Now that you have accomplished the task of finishing this book, and have finished your twelve homework assignments, it is time for your final task. This is the task many people stop at after reading the book and doing their other homework.

Your final homework is to implement all of the changes you've learned, or at least as many as possible. You must go out there and do your best to avoid falling back into that vicious debt cycle. Work on building your savings, work on making the changes that will help lead you to the life you most want to live. Now, good luck!